THE WONDER OF
UNICORNS

"When I first read *The Wonder of Unicorns*, I couldn't put the book down — it spoke directly to my soul and helped me to bring my visions into the world! If you want to dive deep into (re-)connecting with these beautiful celestial beings, the unicorns, I truly recommend this unique book with its high frequency and its wonderful and life-changing meditations, exercises, and rituals. You can also feel Diana's pure light and grace pouring through every single page."

— ISABELLE VON FALLOIS, author of *The Power of Your Angels*

"The light-filled energy of the unicorns pulses through this book. It's a treasure trove, densely packed with metaphysical and historical context, anecdotal evidence of their presence, and transformative influence. Detailed exercises are given for practical application on how to work with these soul guardians, increasingly present to assist humanity in this era. A must-have manual for modern times."

— DAWN BROWN, spiritual coach, healer,
and author of *Chibi Anime Angel Cards*

"Diana Cooper has again paved the way for our helpers from higher dimensions with original and timeless work, exploring the energy and origins of the unicorns. These souls are the most powerful we will ever encounter, and incredible changes occur when they enter our lives. Read this book to learn how and why!"

— TIM WHILD, coauthor of *The Archangel Guide to Ascension*

"Diana Cooper's *The Wonder of Unicorns* is a life-changing book that has opened my eyes to the magical kingdom of these amazing high-frequency beings. It has brought into my life three amazing unicorn guides who are helping me step more and more into my power and align more and more with my soul mission. Much gratitude."

— FRANZISKA SIRAGUSA, principal teacher with the Diana Cooper
School of White Light and author of *Higher Ascension Tools*

THE WONDER OF
UNICORNS

Ascending with the Higher Angelic Realms

DIANA COOPER

ILLUSTRATED BY DAMIAN KEENAN

 FINDHORN PRESS

Findhorn Press
One Park Street
Rochester, Vermont 05767
www.findhornpress.com

Findhorn Press is a division of Inner Traditions International

Disclaimer
The content of this book is given in good faith and intended for information only.
Neither author nor publisher can be held liable by any person for any loss or
damage whatsoever which may arise directly or indirectly from the use of this
book or any of the information therein.

ISBN 978-1-62055-983-3 (print)
ISBN 978-1-62055-984-0 (ebook)

Printed and bound in the United States by Versa Press, Inc.

10 9 8 7 6 5 4 3 2

Edited by Michael Hawkins
Text design, layout, and illustrations by Damian Keenan
This book was typeset in Minion Pro and Calluna Sans
with Trajan Pro used as a display typeface.

To send correspondence to the author of this book, mail a first-class letter to
the author c/o Inner Traditions • Bear & Company, One Park Street, Rochester,
VT 05767, USA and we will forward the communication, or contact the author
directly at **https://dianacooper.com**

I dedicate this book to my grandchildren,
Isabel and Finn, with much love.

I acknowledge and thank all those
who have generously told me their stories
and allowed me to share them.

Most of all I thank the Unicorns
for their patience and light.

CONTENTS

PREFACE

Time has flown past since that day in 2007 when the unicorns first came to me. I remember the feeling of surprise as this pure white energy appeared silently and suddenly behind me and how still I felt. I learnt that day that the unicorns are seventh-dimensional ascended horses, that they are angelic beings and that they used to be with us during the high-frequency time of Atlantis.

The unicorn being said that at last the energy of humanity was rising again so that thousands of unicorns were reconnecting to us. That was twelve years ago and since then there have been astonishing and unprecedented changes on Earth. By raising our consciousness we have earned the right for the current wave of unicorns to touch everyone on the planet.

They told me that the unicorns were here to bring enlightenment to humanity. Currently, we see with blinkered eyes from a limited viewpoint. The unicorns want to help us to see all perspectives with the eyes of an eagle who surveys the world with vast, all encompassing, yet piercingly clear vision.

When we understand the challenges that others face, we will have new respect and compassion for our fellow humans and animals. We will see with eyes of oneness. To help bring this about the unicorns, who are known to be the purest of the pure, are influencing us by dissolving lower energies. They pour high-frequency white light onto us and when we absorb it, this transforms us. Their very presence is a blazing light that illuminates who we truly are.

This Is What They Can Do for You

Unicorns are also soul healers who can release ancient traumas of the soul, so that you can find deep inner contentment and happiness. They can transmute pain from your past lives and other parts of your soul journey. They enable you to see your divine essence, who you really are, so that you can stand in your true magnificence. When they touch you at a soul level your light can shine and you can experience soul satisfaction.

They are great healers, who can help you think and feel differently. They touch your third eye and your heart with their incredible light. This raises your frequency above the mental and emotional sources of dis-ease. If your frequency is higher than that of the illness, it cannot be sustained. It has to disappear.

They work with children and help animals. They also heal your inner child. They give you the energy you need to achieve your mission. When you work with unicorns, people see their light within you and respond accordingly to you.

The unicorn energy has poured into Earth in an unprecedented way and is offering us all a huge opportunity to raise our frequency. Working with angels and dragons, they are taking the planet and us to ascension.

Since that first connection I have often been aware of unicorns round me. They have also poured their extraordinary light over me and raised my spirits. In meditations and visualizations they have carried me into totally awesome places and I know they have accelerated my ascension.

Other people have seen them with me and clairvoyants have often shared that they perceive them with me during seminars, above my car when I arrive somewhere or generally near me. I feel so blessed!

Unicorns and the Moon

If you had an incarnation in the Golden Era of Atlantis, and almost everyone reading these words will have done so, you will also have linked into the unicorns on your long soul journey.

Until 2015, the unicorns stepped into this Universe through Lakumay, the ascended aspect of Sirius. Many of you have also entered Earth through this planet and will therefore have already connected at a soul level with these pure beings.

The third way you may be linked with the unicorns, without even realizing it, is through the Moon. The energy of the Moon has become more powerful in recent years and is flooding our planet with divine feminine light. The unicorns are now entering Earth through this beautiful portal as well as through Sirius. So, if you love the Moon, you will find it easy to meet them.

My little dog, Venus, absolutely loves to sit outside in the garden in the moonlight. In fact, I find it hard to get her to come inside at full moon. She bathes in the light and is very quiet in the hope that I don't notice her. Because I know that she is communicating with the unicorns and other Illumined Ones at these times, I try not to disturb her. The pure and simple hearts of animals enable them to talk easily with the unicorns.

It is not only beautiful to be flooded by moonlight. It is also magical. The unicorns use the silvery light to make wondrous things happen. During this enhanced moon energy tell the unicorns of your dreams and expect them to come true. It is a wonderful time to hold a ceremony and call on the unicorns to make it more potent. If you can meditate in the moonlight, think of unicorns and just know that they are touching you. They can transform your life. Amazingly, as I was typing these words a butterfly flew into my conservatory, round me, and out again. I felt it was reminding me just how important it is to call in unicorns during moonlight ceremonies.

The full moon is an excellent time to create a unicorn portal. You can even build a column of light from the moon into your garden or your home and dedicate it as a high-frequency gateway through which unicorns can enter. You will feel the shift in energy. For more information, there is a chapter on creating ritual and ceremony with the unicorns in this book.

Unicorn Blessings

The other day I was asked, "If you just had one ascension tool what would it be?" I did not even think. Out of my mouth jumped, "Unicorn blessings!" I feel that offering unicorn blessings brings great light into you. You can give them anywhere, at any time. When I am walking the dogs, I love to bless the trees and all of nature with unicorn energy. It makes a difference. I even send unicorn wisdom blessings to world leaders when they are making decisions that do not align with the new paradigm of peace, cooperation, and oneness.

In the twelve years since this book was first released the frequency of our planet has risen enormously. We are all now on an accelerated ascension journey and the unicorns, with many other great beings of light, have been instrumental in this process. Currently, there are many ninth-dimensional and even ineffable tenth-dimensional unicorns pouring their light into Earth and particularly touching those who are ready. I believe this book will enable you to connect with these wondrous unicorns. This will enable your twelve fifth-dimensional chakras to light up and blaze higher light.

In this book I share information the unicorns have given me about who they are, why they are flocking to Earth now and how they can help us. I explain how you can connect with them and open yourself up to their healing and their pure light. I share experiences I have had with them and also those of other people. And you will find meditations and exercises to help you find your personal connection with them.

I love the unicorns. They have transformed my life and I believe brought about a metamorphosis in me. I hope this book will enable you to meet them and experience their love and assistance in your life.

Diana Cooper
July 2019

INTRODUCTION
THE UNICORNS ARRIVE

Some years ago I was sitting quietly on the lawn of my beautiful garden, relaxing in a chair and thinking about *The Web of Light*, the last of my spiritual trilogy that I was in the process of writing. Gradually I became aware of a being near me and a wonderful sense of stillness enveloped me. I was aware it was an angelic presence but it was not an angel. And then it burst into my consciousness: a unicorn was with me! I felt very still and serene. Everything was silent. Nothing moved. Time stood still.

The unicorn that came to me that day did not have a shape. It was a white light. Gradually its thoughts appeared in my mind and I knew it was communicating. It told me that it was indeed a unicorn and it had seen my light and wanted to work with me. Oh!

It told me it wanted me to write about unicorns in my book. I gulped, not sure how they would fit in. However, many years before when the angels asked me to write about them I had declined on the grounds that I didn't know anything about them and people would think I was mad!

At that time the angels asked me if my ego was doing my work or my higher self and I quickly revoked my refusal and accepted their incredible offer. I never regretted it and was not going to make the same mistake again!

I knew nothing about unicorns other than that they were mythical horses, which was even less than I knew about angels all those years ago. So I telepathically imparted this to the unicorn, who downloaded information into my consciousness, like a cosmic transfer.

It told me that they were etheric beings, seventh-dimensional ascended horses, fully of the angelic realms. It said they had been present in Atlantis during the Golden Times, when everyone was able to connect to them, just as they did to their guardian angel. At that time, everyone had their own personal unicorn who stayed with them and helped to hold their frequency high. But when the civilization of Atlantis declined, the unicorns had to withdraw as they could not reach down to such a low level of frequency.

All those years ago, when the angels asked me to write and talk about them, they said that angels were flocking to the planet under directive from Source to help raise the consciousness of everyone and help Earth to ascend. I wondered if it would now be the same with the unicorns.

The unicorn immediately responded that they have reappeared in response to the prayers of humanity for help. And now enough people have raised their frequency to a sufficiently high level to make this possible, so they are gradually coming back to bring enlightenment to those who are ready. Unicorns purify us, for their purpose is to trigger the innocence of the divine self, that essence we had the moment we became a divine spark.

They Remind Us of Who We Truly Are

Dutifully, and I have to say, joyfully, I started to weave them into the story of *The Web of Light*. A week later, I left the UK for France to facilitate an Angel and Ascension teacher training course for the Diana Cooper School. On the plane I thought to myself, I must focus on angels and ascension. I won't mention unicorns.

The course was held in a beautiful hotel, surrounded by fields and next door to a stable. On the first morning I could scarcely believe it when magnificent pure white horses galloped up and down the field outside our room! What a sign from the Universe!

Of course, I soon found myself talking about unicorns and as I did so, they gave me more and more information. Their energy was so strong that everyone on the course formed a profound connection with them.

Unicorns were coming into my life in a big way. I was aware of them all the time. They were in the woods when I walked. They were often in the garden. Clairvoyants saw them behind me on the platform when I was lecturing. I really felt I needed to write a book about them but I had little information.

One evening a friend called at my house. Kathy is a medium and we chatted about our visions for the future. As we did so, Mother Mary came in. Now I am very close to Mother Mary and she has often helped me. On this occasion, she came in to tell me she wanted me to write a book for her but she said firmly and very decisively, the unicorn book was very important and must come first. She asked me to get on with it!

When I pointed out that I was happy to do so but did not know enough about unicorns, she told me to spend a week with them. "Ok," I replied, mentally flipping through my diary, which was absolutely full. Somehow I would have to find time. And I did.

So who are they, these seventh-dimensional creatures of myth and magic? Why are they here now? How can they help us? How can we learn to work with them? How do they differ from angels?

I answer all these questions and share my own and other people's experiences with them. I discuss some of the ancient myths and legends and try to interpret them from a higher spiritual perspective. And I include exercises, meditations and games that you might find helpful to enable you to connect with them.

The unicorns have taught me such a lot. I feel overwhelming love, respect and awe for them and hope that you too will feel touched by their energy and their love as you read their book.

CHAPTER 1

ABOUT UNICORNS

U nicorns are fully of the angelic realms and live in the seventh dimension, the seventh heaven. They are aspects of the divine, in the same way that angels are. They are white horses, which have ascended into the higher dimensions. Just like humans, horses reincarnate until they become perfected beings. In their case, they return to Earth again and again to learn their lessons, until they become white horses and can ascend in a blaze of light. Then these horses work with us in their spiritual bodies as unicorns.

While angels work through the heart,
unicorns work with the soul.

Angels help and guide their human charges in all sorts of ways. They smooth our paths and respond to requests as long as they are for the highest good. They guard and protect those in their care and whisper higher choices to them. Their wings enfold, comfort and succour their charges.

The great ascended horses on the other hand look for those who radiate a light and have a vision beyond their little selves. They seek people who aspire to help others and to change the world for the better, even if it is just their small corner of it.

The light of a unicorn is so powerful that it enters
people gradually, in waves, only ever as much as an
individual can cope with at any time.

They help you hold your vision and give you courage and faith to continue in the face of challenges and opposition. They strengthen and steady you, so that you have the dignity and charisma to fight for what you believe is right. Unicorns grant wishes. Angels do this too for they grant wishes of the heart, those things that make you feel happier and lighter.

Unicorns grant soul wishes, those things that satisfy you deeply and help you fulfil your pre-life contract.

They encourage you to hold on to your aspirations and visions, to stand up for those ambitions that are for the highest good of all. They have the long-term growth of your soul, your community and the world in mind.

Clairvoyants see unicorns as shining white horses with a spiralling horn of light from their brow chakra, the chakra of enlightenment. One psychic told me that when she saw a unicorn it was like seeing a million diamonds sparkling in the sunlight, so bright that she could scarcely look at it.

Their horn can be likened to a magic wand, pouring out divine energy. Wherever they direct this light, healing takes place. This is not just physical and emotional healing but also soul healing. They dissolve and heal the deepest, most profound wounds of the soul, which may have plagued you for many lifetimes. If you are ready the unicorns can help you clear all that karma, whether these are personal, family or country lessons. You can call on them to help.

One of the most wondrous sights is to see the Lords of Karma, who are of the angelic rank of Powers, cross the heavens as they perform their duties, surrounded by hundreds of unicorns. Powers vibrate at a frequency far beyond the archangels and are mighty lights.

Unicorns reconnect people to their spirit. When you think about a unicorn it wakens an energy within you that aligns you to higher realms. And if you meet a unicorn in dreams or meditations, your soul is connecting to the unicorn energy and great changes take place. Behind the scenes they are inspiring you.

The unicorns carry qualities of love, peace, calm, gentleness, hope, majesty, caring, magic and mystery. They will come to you when you are ready, helping you too to develop your unicorn qualities. Of course, they work in cooperation with animals as well as the angels and elementals.

While they are perfectly balanced in their male and female qualities, they are considered to carry feminine energy. This is because wisdom, compassion and love are more powerful than masculine qualities.

While angels take people's prayers and the wishes of their hearts to God, the unicorns, working at a soul level, take the soul longing of individuals to the Creator and enable great visions to be fulfilled. Sometimes these longings are like the flicker of a candle but the unicorns see them and fan them with their breath to try to ignite the sparks into flames. In this way the aims and aspirations of some of the greatest people have been brought forward.

Sometimes, while people are in their physical bodies, they are hardly aware of the dreams their souls aspire to or the extraordinary opportunities open to them. They are literally sleep walking through their lives. A unicorn will occasionally visit such a person in his dreams and try to wake him up. When they succeed, that individual's life will change overnight.

One of the greatest gifts you can have in this life is to connect with your magnificent unicorn.

EXERCISE: Ask the Unicorns for Help

If you could do something monumental in your life that would help the world what would you do? If you knew you could do it, what would be the first step? How could you take just that one small step?

Ask the unicorns to help you do it.

CHAPTER 2

MEETING YOUR UNICORN

In order to meet your unicorn you need to attract it to you. Everything in creation is subject to the Laws of Attraction.

If you wish to draw wealth to you, you must absorb yourself in prosperous thoughts and if you want lots of friends, you must radiate warmth, friendship and generosity. If you want to be happy you must do things that make you feel joyful. So if you really want to meet your unicorn you must think about them, imagine them, talk of them and immerse yourself in unicorn energies. These are innocence, purity, happiness, love and other beautiful qualities. The most important of all is a desire to serve.

If you often think about unicorns and you have a desire to help the world, a unicorn will soon be with you.

When you relax and trust this, you will find you are being nudged in the right direction and new ideas will come, popped into your mind by the unicorns. You will also have a greater sense of confidence and a feeling that you really can make a difference, until your desire to do something constructive to help others will become stronger.

Slowly you will start to sense, feel or know that a unicorn is helping you. Maybe you will find a little white feather to indicate that one has come to you, for unicorns leave feathers just as angels do. Or they may give you another clue.

For example, Evadne was telling a friend of mine that she had an idea, which would enable her to help children in schools. After their discussion, all the way home she considered her vision wondering if the unicorns would help bring her plan to fruition. When she arrived home her little daughter had found a unicorn picture and traced it for her. Evadne had an overwhelming rush of joy and knew this was a sign from the unicorns.

Many people meet their unicorn during meditation, in other words in their inner world. If you go to a high-energy place where the veils are thin, such as a waterfall, mountaintop or forest glade, and allow yourself to be still, you may even catch a glimpse of one.

Glamour and Illusion

Glamour and illusion are the downfalls of all spiritual work. It is so exciting to connect with other realms and dimensions that people can get carried away. This is why many religions frown upon meditation and psychic work.

People often become euphoric when they meet their unicorns, which is wonderful as long as they are sensible. These great beings of light will illuminate your path and help you attain your soul purpose.

However, if you place ridiculous expectations or projections onto them, they will simply withdraw. This leaves a void into which a lesser entity can slide, pretending to be a unicorn. Such a low being can lead you on a merry dance, feeding you false information mixed with truth, which inevitably leads to confusion at the very least. If you maintain a high spiritual intent, remain grounded and use common sense, you will never be deluded in this way.

I have to confess that in my early days on my spiritual path I was occasionally hoodwinked by this. Luckily I am pretty grounded but I was singed a couple of times and learnt to be very mindful.

Glamour is when you allow yourself to be drawn away from the purity of the divine by the allure of the beings you meet and the otherworldly experiences you have. Illusion is where you muddle truth with false imagination and projection.

Angels, guides, unicorns and Masters are divine beings. Healing, channelling and readings are links to the divine. These inspirational beings and experiences can all help you on your spiritual path, comfort you, expand your conscious awareness, heal and encourage you, but like all powerful things must be treated with respect and care. It is better to access them in addition to your meditation practices, not instead of.

*Your link to your still, quiet centre, where you listen to
the voice of God, is your safeguard and your strength.*

A Unicorn Always Speaks of Love

Unicorns and angels always come from the highest spiritual perspective. If something is urging you to fight, hurt or harm another or act in any way dishonestly, it is not unicorn energy. Disregard it, purify yourself with the gold and silver violet flame and ground yourself. Then you can tune into the unicorns again, who will impress noble, aspirational and peaceful thoughts onto you.

Remember to Ask

If you ask your unicorn to help you, you do not by-pass God, for the unicorns and their Creator have a direct communication at all times. Like angels, the unicorns do not have free will, so they will never do or suggest anything other than the divine intention for you. Nor will they contravene the will of your soul.

Unicorns Are Pure White Light

Your unicorn is a being of pure white light. Because it is so pure and bright, it could blind or overwhelm you, so it will always tone its energy down to the level you can bear. It would never shine more light onto you than you can cope with.

Currently, everything is changing as more unicorns come into the planet. They have sent in such a huge wave of energy that their images are everywhere. Children love them. People talk about them. Few realize that they are real beings who answer prayers and can make a difference to their lives. But the wave of understanding is getting stronger.

You only have to think of a spiritual being and it takes one thousandth of a second for it to be with you. I was pondering this one day when I was walking my dogs in a local park. As a mother walked past me pushing her toddler in a pushchair, he dropped his toy unicorn. As she picked it up she said to him, "You've dropped your unicorn." I immediately saw the flash of white light as a unicorn was with them. For an instant it lit them up and I realized that the unicorns have chosen to make their presence felt in this way, so that they can touch millions of people each day. No wonder the frequency everywhere is rising.

A Unicorn Journal

It is helpful to create a unicorn journal. Choose a special book and decorate it if you wish to. Dedicate it to your experiences and impressions with your unicorn. The more you write, the closer your connection will become. If you date each entry, when you look back in the future you may be amazed at the spiritual journey they have helped you undertake.

Preparing to Meet Your Unicorn

One way to meet your unicorn is during a meditative visualization, when the light around you is calm and clear.

Alternatively, because unicorns love peaceful places in nature, you may like to meditate outside in a quiet spot, especially where there is the sound of flowing water. Let the singing of birds and the rustle of leaves be your music. If you are meditating indoors find a place where you can be quiet and undisturbed. A candle dedicated to your intention for meeting your unicorn helps to raise the energy, as does spiritual music or joss sticks.

E X E R C I S E : Visualization to Meet Your Unicorn

1. Close your eyes and breathe comfortably in and out of your heart centre for a while.
2. Place a ball of shimmering white reflective light around you, so that only pure unicorn energy can enter.
3. Then breathe in love and breathe out peace until you feel relaxed.
4. Picture yourself sitting in a peaceful, safe place by a beautiful lake. Imagine moonlight shining onto the water. Take time to listen to the sounds. Breathe in the perfumes of the evening air.
5. Through the moonlight you see a silver white light moving towards you and out of it emerges a magnificent unicorn.
6. The illumined creature walks towards you and stops in front of you, lighting you up with its glow.
7. Sense the love flowing from it to you.
8. The unicorn bows its head and directs light from its horn into your heart. Take time to feel this, like a flame of love entering you.

9. If you wish you may stand and stroke your unicorn.
10. Look into its eye to make soul-to-soul contact.
11. Spend a little time getting to know your unicorn.
12. Ask it to telepathically impart any message it has for you. Listen.
13. Thank it and watch it walking away through the moonlight.
14. Open your eyes.
15. Record anything you experienced in your unicorn journal.

Remember you can do this visualization as many times as you like and you can take your friends and family through it too.

CHAPTER 3

How Unicorns Help

Protection

I was talking to my friend Liz Roe French, who is an excellent astrologer, medium and healer, on the phone and she told me that she had been clearing energies in a big old house in Yorkshire. She said it was on a powerful ley line and there was work to be done on many levels, so during her stay she had started to clear the stuck energy.

As she worked she became aware of a huge peach and gold light above the building, like a cloud. And then she saw six unicorns walking round the cloud, clearly protecting the work she had done. A few days later when she tuned in there was only one unicorn but he was evidently on duty for he was prancing lightly around the area.

Duncan Gemel told me that he was under psychic attack. He immediately called in his two unicorns, Starlight and Solerius, and psychically saw a white flash and their shoulders as they charged to his rescue. They later told him that his lesson was to ask for help.

Support

When you are drooping in a long supermarket queue or waiting for a train, be aware of your unicorn. He may well be standing by you, ready to take the strain off you. While he may be invisible to you, you will feel his energy if you surrender and let him support you. Be careful. This is not physical support, so you may well fall onto the floor if you lean on him! However, he will offer energetic refreshment, which will lift you physically.

Communication

When your unicorn wishes to draw attention to his presence he may well nudge you! Many people have reported that they have felt a physical nudge as if a horse has pushed them even though they are in the middle of nowhere or are in the shopping centre. If you think it is your unicorn, trust that it is! Use your energy to connect and listen rather than wonder or doubt if you imagined it.

Immediately quieten your breathing and draw your senses away from the outside world of hustle and bustle. Even though you are in a noisy place, you can find inner quiet. Then you can be alert to the messages from your unicorn. These will probably come as flashes or thoughts or gut feelings. With me they often download a whole chunk of information into my mind. When you receive answers, honour and act on them.

Inspiration

Truda Clark and Susan Venus went with a friend to give reiki healing to an elderly lady who lived out in the wilds of the country. Truda told me that she lived in rather a spooky overgrown cottage with a paddock next to it in which lived four wild horses, which had never been ridden.

The healing session took a long time, so that it was dark when they finished. The lady to whom they had been giving healing said to them: "Would you like to see my unicorn?" Surprised they replied: "Oh you mean a picture of a unicorn, do you?" "No, a real one," the lady responded. "Come with me." Intrigued Truda and Susan followed the lady out into the paddock. This is what they wrote about the experience.

"It was one of those special nights—the air was cool and still. We approached the gate, the field beyond lost in darkness. As our eyes adjusted to the change between the lights shining softly from the windows of the nearby house, we acknowledged the wonder of a perfect night sky. Between and above the towering trees, the stars were amazingly bright. Lorraine softly called her horses. You could feel their presence, even before their answering whinnies reached our ears. We waited with a strong sense that this was their space—their time—we were only onlookers, duly privileged to be there.

Without warning they came out of the darkness—on the left a darker, smaller form, eyes bright, head up, and by its side a white majestic creature. It took our breath away. We clung to each other with awe and delight. The faint blur of feathered wings, the swift sight of a horn between warm knowing eyes, all captured within a brief moment in time. A truly magical moment. Plunging into the light, there came a unicorn!"

Assistance

Kathy runs a development group. They were sitting in a circle intent on their work when she looked up and saw that they were totally surrounded by unicorns, there to help everyone move forward.

I heard a similar story after a session at an Atlantis Week workshop. This particular group were connecting to their unicorns by singing. At the end they looked up and every one of them saw a group of unicorns in the sky, circling above them.

Companionship

Ever done something alone and felt you wanted a friend to be with you? Call on your unicorn. They are often seen accompanying a lonely traveller and they may even join you in a shopping mall if you really need them.

Answering Questions

I had a very interesting letter from Laura, who had just changed her career to consciousness coaching, at the age of 50. During a meditation in which we connected to our unicorns and called on them for assistance, she discovered he was called Unec. She decided to ask Unec for confirmation that her life change was correct.

First she asked: "Have I done the right thing by changing careers?" The answer came with a profound nod of his head, up and down, up and down. She then said: "For this to happen I need quite a bit of money which I haven't got at this stage." His answer came again in a vigorous nod up and down as if he wanted to gallop on one spot.

Laura knew that she had made the right decision and was getting all the support she needed from the unicorns and angels.

Receiving the Title *The Wonder of Unicorns*

As I was walking along the beach on a beautiful November day I was mulling over the title for this book. For some reason, I had become dissatisfied with my working title and the alternative I had decided on. With the sea breeze on my face I was very aware of the unicorns around me and was thinking how much they had helped me.

Suddenly, from nowhere, a new title, *The Wonder of Unicorns,* dropped into my mind. The more I contemplated it the more right it felt. I decided to sit on a bench and ask the unicorns for help, so I found a piece of paper in my bag and tore it into four. On each piece I wrote one of the possible titles—*Unicorn Magic, A Little Light on Unicorns, The Wonder of Unicorns,* and on the last one I placed a cross, in case the unicorns wanted a different title altogether and to give them the choice.

I screwed the papers up and shuffled them, held them between the palms of my hands and asked the unicorns to indicate their preference. As I touched one piece of paper I had a sense of four unicorns in front of me shaking their heads. When I touched the next one they all nodded. At the third and fourth they shook their heads. I repeated it again to check and had the same impressions.

For a second I felt absurdly nervous as if this was tremendously important. When I opened the second piece of paper and read *The Wonder of Unicorns* I had the most overpowering feeling of joy and rightness. So that is how this book received its title.

EXERCISE: Ask for Help with a Decision

STEP 1: Decide on your question. You may well find that as you are thinking about your possible answers, one will stand out to you. In that case of course you have received your help already. Assuming this is not the case you may like to write down your question though this is not essential. It just helps clarity.

STEP 2: Write possible answers or solutions onto separate pieces of paper. Make sure you leave one blank in case none of these is desirable. Then screw or fold each of them up and shuffle them.

STEP 3: Now create a sacred space into which the unicorns can come. Here are some beautiful ways you can do this.

1. Raise the energy of the room or place outside with music or a singing bowl.
2. Light a circle of candles and sit in the middle.
3. Place your hands in the Namaste position holding the folded up papers between your palms.

4. Silently or aloud invoke the unicorns and ask them to indicate in some way that paper which bears the highest possible solution to your problem.
5. Touch each piece of paper. You may sense a tingle with one of them. You may picture the unicorns in front of you and receive an indication with a nod or shake. You may simply receive a 'prompting' to pick one of them.
6. Read your optimum answer.
7. Thank the unicorns for their help.

CHAPTER 4

Unicorn Names

Every being whether it is human, animal, fairy, angel or unicorn has a name which carries its unique vibration and helps to connect it to its soul. The vibration of your name brings your soul intention to you. When you call a creature by its name, it enables you to bond more closely with it, just as you feel more connected to someone when you know what they are called. This is why it is so important to say a name with love, for the person receives the love at the deepest level of their being.

Most humans have everyday names that are used by their friends and family, who can connect with them at that frequency. When they develop spiritually they may discover their spiritual name, which attunes to a higher aspect of their soul. More people are now adopting their spiritual names or allowing certain people to use them.

Often your unicorn will give you its spiritual name immediately. Sometimes it will start by offering you a lower-frequency name, so that you call in part of its energy. When you are ready it will give you its higher name so that you can link into its full power and glory. Either way it is really helpful to personalize your relationship and find out what your unicorn wants you to call it.

If you sit quietly and ask your unicorn to tell you its name, he may drop it into your mind. It will come as a thought but this is how your unicorn telepathically communicates with you.

A Unicorn Called Dobbin

Susan Ann was one of the teachers in the Diana Cooper Angel School. She described how she met her unicorn.

"In 2005, I attended Diana's Mind, Body, Spirit event in London, where Diana introduced me to the audience. After the break Diana led us in a powerful visualization to meet our unicorns and receive their names. Afterwards she asked people to share the names they had received. As they raised their hands I sat at the back of the room wondering what to do. My unicorn had given me the name 'Dobbin'! People were calling out wonderful and glorious names. How could I say my unicorn was called Dobbin? It was deeply embarrassing! I kept quiet.

"Over the following months I established a powerful connection with Dobbin. Then, one day he told me his real name was Aurora and I have used that name with him ever since. Now when I tell people about Dobbin I can laugh for I realize it was an important learning for me. My ego was brought down to Earth by being given a name that I felt was silly and unbecoming. It showed me that anybody can receive an 'ordinary' name, it doesn't have to be something flowery or flamboyant. I still worked with Dobbin though and deepened my link with him despite his name.

"A couple of years later, I was sitting with Diana in a taxi on the way to an airport. I relayed this story to her, emphasizing how much I resonated with the name Aurora. 'Look,' she said suddenly, pointing to a hotel we were passing. It was called Aurora Hotel. I took this as an indication that my unicorn was with me listening to the story and probably having a little smile to himself. "

One Horn, One Country

Unicorns are called "one horn" in most countries and languages and the list below gives a fascinating insight into the differences.

English	Unicorn
Russian	Yedinorog
Lithuanian	Vienaragis
Portuguese and Spanish	Unicornio
Swedish	Enhorning
Finnish	Yksisarvinen
Hebrew	Had-KerenHe

Norwegian	Enhjorning
Romanian	Inorog
Arabic	Karkadann
Esperanto	Unukornulo
Latvian	Vienradzis
Latin	Unicornis
Polish	Jednorozec
Greek	Monokeros
Dutch	Eenhoorn
German	Einhorn
French	Licorne
Italian	Alicorno or Licorno
Welsh	Uncorn
Persian	Karkadann
Japanese	Ki-rin or Sin-you
Chinese	Ch'I lin or K'i-lin

Diana's Unicorn

My unicorn's name is Elfrietha. It took a few attempts to receive it correctly, mainly due to my preconceived idea that the name was Elfrieda. I kept receiving a shake of the head, a 'no!' until I ventured 'Elfrietha?' at which there was a sigh of relief. The unicorns do have great patience.

EXERCISE: To Find Your Unicorn's Name
Indoors

1. Sit quietly where you will not be disturbed.
2. Light a candle to raise your frequency.
3. Breathe comfortably until you feel relaxed.
4. Visualize yourself in a beautiful place out in nature.
5. Ask your unicorn to come into the scene. You may see or sense this.
6. Thank your unicorn for coming to you.
7. Ask it for the name it wants to be known by.
8. Be receptive to whatever comes in.

Outdoors

1. Walk outside in nature, somewhere quiet and beautiful.
2. Allow yourself to relax. Listen to the sounds and breathe in the smell of nature. Feel the earth under your feet as you move along.
3. Look around you. As you relax you may be aware of a unicorn.
4. Mentally invite your unicorn to walk with you.
5. Whether you can see it or not, know that your unicorn is close.
6. Ask it for the name it wants to be known by.
7. As you walk quietly on, allow the unicorn's name to float into your mind.

CHAPTER 5

UNICORN CONNECTIONS

Unicorns make their presence known in many different ways. Sometimes they appear to you but more often they let you know they are around in some other way.

A lady came up to me at the end of a seminar. She sounded absolutely thrilled as she said; "When you took us on a meditation to meet our unicorns, mine told me he was called Star. You have just signed my book, 'follow your star!' "

I guess her unicorn was talking into my ear.

The late Donald McKinney, author of *Walking in the Mist*, told me that he was in his shop, Body and Soul, talking to a customer. They were discussing all things spiritual, when suddenly she said: "You'll think I'm mad when I tell you this. You'll never believe what happened to me. I was walking in the Highlands of Scotland in the early morning. There was a low mist lying and suddenly a unicorn emerged from the mist. It stood in front of me and bowed, acknowledging me." She said that nothing like that had ever happened to her before and that it felt like a magical experience. It affirmed to her that there is wonder in the world.

Agnes McCluskey, who is a colour therapist and a very spiritual and psychic lady, described her brother as a big hairy biker. Nevertheless he was clearly open to unicorn guidance, for one day he was in a New Age shop where he saw a china unicorn. It literally said to him, "Take me to Agnes." So he bought it and gave it to her. She still has it and recognizes that the unicorns were connecting with her brother and with herself.

I was delighted to meet Laura Cameron Jackson and Lyn McNicol at their Lunicorn stall at an exhibition. They shared with me how their company came about. Neither had been satisfied with her job and they were drawn together by their fascination with unicorns, fairies and the elemental kingdoms. For a long time they had been discussing what they could do that would satisfy their souls.

One day, Laura was on a coach, which passed through several villages, when out of the window she saw a pub called The Unicorn. It felt like a sign and at that moment, in a burst of inspiration, the unicorn idea came.

Now they devote their lives to helping children and adults connect with unicorns and giving them hope. They run unicorn parties and workshops for children, who love unicorns. They told me: "When we say, 'Who believes in unicorns?', the youngsters all say, 'We do' and if they ask, 'Has anyone seen one?' there are always two or three children who can describe those they have seen."

Laura met her unicorn through her guide, Ashon, who is a very serious twelfth century monk. It happened like this. While she was in a meditative state the monk said, "Come, my dear." He took her hand and led her along a path—and there stood her unicorn, Wanderer, waiting for her! That was her first encounter with a unicorn.

Laura also has a very mischievous baby unicorn that appeared one day with Wanderer. Once the baby suddenly said, "Here's Charger," and a new unicorn with very powerful energy and amazing eyes appeared, running. Clearly she is very connected with the unicorn kingdom and they are working closely with her.

Lyn has a forthright unicorn guide called Jasminda. He communicates with her in quite direct and strict terms and pulls her up. For example, one day he told her that she had an appalling diet and must put it right! She took him very seriously. But like all higher-dimensional beings he also encourages her work.

Everyone thought they were crazy to give up good jobs and pensions to spread the light of unicorns and they were beginning to doubt their decision. One wintry afternoon, Lyn was feeling exhausted. She was sitting in front of a blank wall in the rest area of a call centre and the lights were on. Suddenly to the left, the lights on the wall formed the shape of a unicorn's head. This light moved forwards and back but always retained its shape. It was the confirmation they needed and it renewed their determination to continue with their mission.

It was such a pleasure to meet Lyn and Laura at their Lunicorn stall and experience the enthusiasm and joy with which they are spreading unicorn light.

❧

Here is another story, from Mary Thomson, about how she met her unicorns during a meditation. "I attended your talk in Glasgow today and thought I'd send you this reflective account of the meditation where we were to meet our unicorn. I saw a stream running through a beautiful forest. An impressive large brown horse appeared at the other side of the water. I heard a voice tell me I was not ready to meet my unicorn yet. I accepted this and moved forward and stroked the horse along his neck. He was a strong yet gentle creature. I felt quite satisfied and privileged to have met him, when suddenly I was standing in the middle of a pool of water surrounded by several unicorns—all glowing white and surrounded by white light. One of the unicorns came to me and let me stroke his neck and mane and a voice in my head said, 'His name is Urbill.'" I find it interesting that she accepted the guidance that she was not yet ready to meet the unicorns and did not resist it. Her acceptance made her ready.

❧

Flavia-Kate was with her husband in Hastings when she acquired a beautiful unicorn soft toy. She instantly fell in love with it and started thinking about unicorns, even having a small one tattooed on her lower back. She wrote: "That was it; I was then visited by the unicorns in my dreams. I had drawn the unicorns to me, without consciously realizing—of course, like attracts like! Their recruitment drive worked and the unicorns then surrounded me as I went about my daily life." She added that they told her that they have recruited her to recruit others to work with them and it was happening with quite a speed. She was aware that people who are meant to work with them are suddenly remembering their passion for unicorns and are asking to be attuned to their energy to help with the healing process on this planet.

She gave me two instances of people who had awakened to their knowing of unicorns. In one case she mentioned the unicorns at her meditation group and explained that they were coming in droves to this planet now to help with the changing energies and ascension process.

A lady, in her mid thirties, told her that she had adored unicorns as a child and thought of them constantly through her teens. She showed her a tattoo of a unicorn on her shoulder that was done when she was 18 years old. After that she hadn't thought of them until now. She became very enthusiastic about them and now her 13-year-old daughter has discovered her own unicorn guide and sees and speaks to her often in a matter of fact way, as children often do.

On another occasion when a client came for a reading she picked out a unicorn card and gasped saying that as she was travelling on the bus, she started thinking of unicorns. She could not understand why as she had not thought of them before but she felt an over-whelming love for them.

As Flavia-Kate tuned into her client's energies she could see unicorns around her. They asked her to tell the lady that they wanted her to work with them and to bring them into her healing work.

A Unicorn Orb

The angels helped technologists to develop digital cameras, so that photographs of spiritual beings could be captured on them. They appear in their light bodies as orbs. If you look at a unicorn orb you will be able to absorb unicorn energy and their qualities from the picture. There are some of these awesome orbs on my website *https:// dianacooper.com*.

EXERCISE: Deepen Your Unicorn Connection

Pure innocence is one way to deepen your unicorn connection, which literally means being in your divine essence. So often the centre of our being gets tangled in other people's expectations and desires or our neediness and lack of self-respect.

So, to deepen your connection, first purify your essence.

1. List all the things that stop you being who you truly are or take away your delight in life. These may be fears or feelings you are not worthy. They may be other people's expectations or you may be tangled emotionally or mentally with others. Perhaps you are in a situation, job or a financial prison from which you can see no escape. When you have completed your list, explore the inner journey below.

2. Hold the intention of purifying your essence and deepening your unicorn connection.
3. Find a place where you can be quiet and undisturbed.
4. Close your eyes and imagine a blue cloak of protection round you.
5. Breathe comfortably until you are relaxed and comfortable.
6. You are climbing up a hill. Half way up you see a thicket and go into it. You are quite safe.
7. In the centre of the thicket there is a great cage. Inside it is a person you recognize as yourself, surrounded by brambles and wire and all sorts of rubbish.
8. You find you have the tools and strength to unlock the cage and clear the brambles to set a pure aspect of yourself free.
9. When the inside of the cage is clear, you see that the person inside is shimmering with light. Welcome this aspect of you and let it merge with you. This may feel wonderful or strange.
10. Walk out of the cage and through the thicket.
11. Call Archangel Zadkiel to transmute the thicket, as well as the cage and all it contains in the gold and silver violet flame. Thank him as you watch it all consumed.
12. Then turn towards a silver path that leads up the hill.
13. You see a great white ball of light moving towards you. This too merges with you.
14. Now you can feel, sense or maybe even see your unicorn.
15. Touch it, stroke it, ride it and really get to know it. Take your time.
16. When you feel complete thank your unicorn for coming to you.
17. Open your eyes and return to the room.
18. You may want to record your experience in your unicorn journal.

CHAPTER 6

THE UNICORN HIERARCHY

U nicorns belong to the angelic hierarchy. The elementals, fairies, pixies, gnomes, salamanders, mermaids, undines, sylphs, nymphs and many others are their younger brothers and sisters. They often work with the unicorns and help them by doing simpler tasks. Above them come the angels and some of these are the guardian angels, those who are designated to look after humans during their lives. Other angels also help humans when asked.

The archangels are in charge of the angels and have their own tasks to oversee. The most well known for their work with humanity are Archangels Michael, Raphael, Uriel and Gabriel. Archangel Michael carries the sword of truth and shield of protection, and is known as the protector. He gives courage and strength to people.

Archangel Raphael is the healer angel. He also helps travellers and opens people to abundance. His twin flame is Mary, the divine mother. She and the unicorns have a very close relationship.

Archangel Uriel is in charge of the angels of peace. He sends his angels to troubled places and situations and they help individuals to empower themselves.

Archangel Gabriel wears radiant white for purity. He brings clarity and joy to people and like the unicorns works with pure white light.

The unicorns are at the same level as the archangels. The King and Queen of the unicorns are at an even higher frequency. They have crowns of light at the top of their heads, which are the emanations from their crown chakras. Aeons ago only the King and Queen could reproduce and I discuss this in Chapter 23, "Unicorn Babies". This gift was handed down as others reached a certain level of maturity or light.

The King and Queen rule the kingdom of unicorns because of their great wisdom and light. They have evolved to this high state and are revered, trusted and respected. They receive their instructions directly from the Seraphim or from Source and are in charge of the entire unicorn kingdom.

Part of their task is to hold the frequency of all the unicorns and they do this by keeping the vision of their divine perfection. They also designate which unicorns are to visit Earth and what their tasks are there. Of course, unicorns are working in many universes and dimensions. As the guardians of all souls, they have a vast undertaking.

The King and Queen are in charge of the evolution of the unicorns through service to the divine will. Therefore unicorns have no free will. Their hearts and souls are so pure that they can only follow the light.

There are other ranks, akin to the titles of human royalty, such as Princes or Princesses, earls or dukes, who only attain their titles by the quality of light they carry. They evolve into these positions to support the King and Queen.

White contains all colours. Black, an absence of light, is more enigmatic. It represents the void containing the deepest mysteries or it can indicate darkness and negativity. For example, the earthly symbol of a black horse represents greed, control and power over others.

Pegasus and Unicorn

The unicorn, which is depicted with his third eye open, is an enlightened, all knowing, all seeing, all wise being. Unicorn people are enlightened people, whose third eyes are sharp and clear. This does not necessarily mean they are clairvoyant in the sense of being able to see pictures, colour and light in other dimensions. Many people are claircogniscent: they simply know.

Pegasus is also an ascended white horse who has fully developed his heart centre, so he is seen with wings. Just as angel's wings are emanations of love from their heart centres, so it is with Pegasus. Angel or Pegasus people are those from whom light radiates like wings.

Consciously or unconsciously they can extend their wings and place them round people or animals, bringing peace and a sense of safety to them. The roles of the unicorn and Pegasus are slightly different. The unicorn's is to inspire, give hope, empower and enlighten, while that of the heart centred Pegasus is to comfort succour and enfold.

Once you have connected with the unicorns and Pegasus you need extra purification to reach the King and Queen of unicorns. They can help you enormously in your quest for spiritual growth. I first met them in meditation. As I entered the kingdom of the unicorns, doors opened and massive light came in. I was conducted to the royal beings and offered myself in service. I also requested healing for my wound from Atlantis, which was proving a problem in my throat centre. At that time they told me I was not totally ready to carry and spread the frequency of light, which I wanted to, but I was nearly there and they would hold my energy.

They also helped me understand the problem with my throat and gave me healing for it. A few weeks later they informed me that I was then ready to take out the higher frequency into the world.

Here is a meditation, which you might like to do to enable you to connect with the King and Queen of the unicorns.

MEDITATION: To Meet the King and Queen of the Unicorns

1. Sit quietly in a place where you will not be disturbed.
2. You may like to light a candle or play soft inspirational music.
3. Imagine yourself sitting quietly under a tree, which is in leaf. Around you everything is soft and green.
4. You may be able to hear the birds singing and the breeze rustling the leaves.
5. A pure white light is approaching and a unicorn steps out of it. It has come to take you to the unicorn kingdom.
6. Greet the unicorn respectfully and ask if you may stroke it.
7. The unicorn invites you to ride on its back. This is a great honour and must be accepted with reverence.
8. You may find your guardian angel sits on the unicorn's back behind you.
9. You feel very safe as the unicorn rises up with you over the mountains and through the stars.
10. Ahead you see the vast white pillars of the gates to the unicorn kingdom.
11. As you enter you see many unicorns, all very still and peaceful.
12. A pure white peacock stands in front of you and displays its tail.

13. Several unicorns honour you by surrounding you, and pouring a shower of stars from their horns over you. Then they form a procession.
14. You walk among the unicorns towards an enchanting castle.
15. Many pure white birds fly above you.
16. As you approach the castle you stand still while white light is poured over you to purify you and raise your frequency. Drink it in. Absorb it into every cell.
17. Then you enter the main door and walk with the unicorns into the reception hall.
18. The King and Queen of the unicorns await you. They each have a horn, wings and crowns of light. They are so radiant it almost hurts your eyes.
19. You may approach them and bow or curtsey to honour them.
20. They telepathically ask how they can help you.
21. You may tell them or ask a question.
22. Stay silent and receptive for the answer.
23. Receive the blessing of their light into your third eye.
24. Thank them. Then move backwards out of the hall and return along the path by which you arrived.
25. Say goodbye to the birds and unicorns.
26. Return to where you started, sitting quietly under your tree.
27. When you are ready, open your eyes.

CHAPTER 7

Unicorn Signs

Feathers

I was really surprised when the unicorns told me that because they are of the angelic hierarchy they leave little white feathers just as angels do. They will leave you one to remind you of their presence; to give you hope; to encourage you to keep trying; or just to say they love you and are close to you.

So when you see a little white feather, be aware that the unicorns or the angels have been to visit you.

I have known my friend Andrew Brel, who writes inspired angel music, for many years. At the time of this story he had just finished composing angel and unicorn music, so he had been living and breathing their energy for some time. Apart from music and writing his hobby is tennis, which he practises conscientiously and passionately. He phoned me twice during this particular week agonizing about playing the club champion in a tournament on Saturday. His opponent was a far better player than Andrew, so no one expected him to get a single game. However, something strange happened.

On the day before the important match, Andrew was practising with a friend. He was about to serve when a white feather fluttered down in front of him and he paused to watch its slow descent until it landed beside him. After that he played really well. All evening he kept thinking about that feather. To him it represented the power to win, for the unicorns help people to overcome lower obstacles.

The following afternoon, when the fateful moment arrived for him to play his infinitely skilled and superior opponent, he thought about the feather each time he was about to serve. It became his point of focus as he played shots he had never played before and discovered previously untapped stamina. It was unbelievable. Where did it all come from? He won the first eleven games. The final score was 6-0, 6-1. And he told me that he only lost the last game when he thought, 'How can I humiliate this gentleman in this way. It is terrible for him.'

Andrew was convinced he was inspired and helped by unicorn energy. Soon after I started writing this book I got into the car to visit a friend. Immediately I was aware of a whole team of unicorns in front of me as if they were leading the way. There were at least eight or ten of them. Naturally my friend and I talked about the unicorns and I was thinking about them as I returned home. Suddenly my car went through what felt like a whirlwind of white feathers. It was as if someone had emptied a feather duvet over the vehicle. They were everywhere. Wow! I thought. Are there that many unicorns with me!

∿

A few weeks later, while unicorns were very much on my mind, my wonderful cleaner Michelle said to me: "What do you want me to do with all these feathers I keep finding round the house?" "Do you?" I said in total astonishment. She replied: "They are everywhere and I never know what to do with them because I don't like to vacuum them up." I asked her to pick them up and put them together, and then I would bless them and thank the unicorns and the angels. It doesn't say much for my powers of observation in the house! Admittedly I had seen a few but nowhere near as many as Michelle found. I am now much more aware.

Someone asked me why I thought these particular feathers were from the unicorns. How could I tell? I just felt intuitively that these were from those beautiful beings because I was writing about them. The angels always feel near me but the unicorns had been very close for a few weeks and what better way to indicate their presence? I found it interesting that they made sure someone else drew attention to the feathers that I might have missed.

Unicorn Presents

I notice that there are now more little model unicorns in the shops made of glass, pewter, ceramic and many other materials than I have ever seen before.

My friend Heather, who is 86 years young at the time of writing, has a close relationship with the spiritual realms. She sees and communicates with fairies and some elementals, as well as the angels. Of course, she loves the unicorns.

Her cleaner, Joyce, is a very grounded and sensible lady who has been working for her for many years. Joyce's sister on the other hand is fey and dreamy, creative and artistic. She had no idea of Heather's gifts or interests and in any case had only met her a couple of times.

One day Joyce's sister was standing in a gift shop when she felt as if someone had come up close behind her but there was no one there. Startled she looked up and her eyes lit on a gorgeous china unicorn with a fairy riding on its back. As she saw it, a voice in her head said, 'Heather.' The girl immediately purchased it and had it gift-wrapped. She gave it to her sister to give to Heather, who was absolutely over-joyed for she recognized that it was a present from the unicorns and she really loves and cherishes it.

When Heather told me the story of her unicorn present, her friend Mary, who was with us, remembered another experience. She and Heather were on holiday in Ireland. Mary was driving and Heather glanced out of the window and saw a small child riding bareback on a pony, holding onto its mane as it galloped recklessly across the moors. When Mary and Heather reached the farm at the end of the road, there stood the pony resting after its exertion but no child. There never had been a child for there were none at the farm.

As Heather remembered the sense of excitement and naughtiness of the child on the pony, she realized it was a fairy child. A few days after she told me this, I looked at my early notes about unicorns and found I had written this:

Unicorns are free and can never be saddled or
bridled, but from generosity and love they will often
allow the spirit of a human to ride them.
This is an incredible honour and should never be taken
for granted. Beings from the elemental kingdoms also
ride them on occasion — a fairy for instance.

Other Signs

When unicorns want you to think about them or to draw your attention to their presence they will find a way to do so. Someone may walk past you wearing a unicorn T-shirt. You may pass a unicorn sign over a pub or café. As in Heather's case, someone may give you a model unicorn or a card depicting one. You may find there is a unicorn orb in a photograph that you or a friend has taken. It is always a good idea to keep your eyes open. It makes their task easier!

White Flowers

In one of my earlier books I tell the story of my friend Pauline, who was a widow and a White Eagle healer. She came to my house one afternoon and we went for a walk together for I had something special to show her. It was a beautiful spring day and we wandered along a path through filtered sunshine to a bank where I had seen white violets growing. When Pauline saw them, she gasped and said that a few days ago a medium had told her that her husband would be waiting for her where the white violets grow.

The energy at that spot was amazing and it was only later that I learnt she loved the unicorns and realized that there was a unicorn there too. Now whenever I see a cluster of white violets I think, not just of Pauline, but also about the unicorns and wonder what message they have for me.

I had an e-mail from a friend who had just been to South Africa. She said: "You mention that unicorns love white flowers, especially an exotic lily. Many times I have heard you mention that Nelson Mandela was touched by unicorn energy.

"On my recent trip to South Africa I was very aware of large white flowers growing wild at the sides of the roads but did not know what they were. On a trip to Robben Island, where Nelson Mandela was held for 18 of his 27 years imprisonment, I was able to see one of these flowers close up. It had a beautiful trumpet about 6 inches (15 cms) across. It struck me that it was more than coincidence that this beautiful flower should be growing where he had spent his harshest times. It wasn't until I got home that I discovered it was an Arum Lily."

According to the unicorns, they came in to support Nelson Mandela while he was in prison. He had earned their assistance but was undoubtedly unconscious of this. They helped him to find the strength and fortitude to accept his trials, so that he emerged with dignity as a wise leader.

EXERCISE: Unicorn Signs

For one week, note down every unicorn sign that you see or hear. You may be surprised just how many there are.

CHAPTER 8

THE UNICORN'S
HORN

There are stories in most parts of the world about mystical creatures of hope and aspiration with a single spiralling horn from their third eye, which is the chakra of enlightenment, far sight and wisdom. The spiral creates a vortex or powerful outward thrust of energy and is a feminine symbol, which has the ability to unlock and unleash blockages on all levels. A clockwise spiral puts energy in while an anti-clockwise one draws old energy out.

White and Golden Horns

Sometimes a unicorn is depicted with a white horn and at others with a golden one. I always wondered why. When I asked the unicorns they told me that the more one of them evolves, the deeper the gold of its horn, indicating great wisdom. A young unicorn will have a white horn, which becomes golden white and finally deep gold.

So how do they evolve? Guardian angels evolve as the people they look after grow spiritually. However, unicorns evolve through service, for example the higher the quality of light they can emit from their horns, the greater their level of evolution.

Healing Horns

One common theme to all the myths worldwide is that the unicorn horn has healing abilities and especially the power to dissolve poison, which metaphorically implies they can ward off evil.

The Story of the Poisoned Pool

In one frequently related story from the East the animals in the forest would come down to a water hole to drink. They were all very nervous and frightened of one another. However, one day a serpent slithered down to the lake and hissed his venom over it. When the animals arrived that evening they perceived the poison and dared not drink. One of the creatures was sent to find the unicorn and ask him to help them. As they waited the animals huddled together for protection and they started to communicate with each other. When the magnificent unicorn arrived, he dipped his pure horn into the pool and the poison was neutralized. The animals were able to drink the sweet water again.

This particular tale also demonstrates how the darkness serves the light. In this case when the serpent spread his evil poison, it forced the animals to communicate with each other and cooperate together to send for assistance. They also learn to appreciate the power of goodness.

The Symbol of the Cross

In some versions of the poisoned pool story the unicorn makes the sign of the cross with his horn over the water and this is enough to dissolve the malevolence.

The cross is a potent symbol. When the vertical line is brought downward it brings heaven to earth. The horizontal line drawn across from the left to the right brings the intention, in this case purification, from the unmanifest world to the manifest one.

The Middle Ages

In the Middle Ages the horn of the unicorn became very valuable, as it was known to purify water, negate poison and cure all diseases. In parts of Europe a servant would carry what was believed to be a unicorn horn round the banqueting table and touch all the food and drink to test it for poison.

Huge amounts of money were spent on powdered horn. In the sixteenth century, Queen Elizabeth I is said to have paid £10,000 for a unicorn horn, which was carved into the royal sceptre and is housed in the royal treasury.

Horns and teeth are still used symbolically to protect royal thrones, ceremonial arches and important places. Presumably all of these are the horns or tusks of whales, elephants, rhinoceros, antelope or any other creature that could pass as a unicorn!

Rhinoceros

I do feel the poor old rhinoceros has suffered greatly because humans recall from the records of the collective unconscious that a one-horned creature is a powerful being, which can effect magical healings and purification. Humanity has projected this higher awareness onto a physical animal with one horn. As a result this huge beast has been hunted for its horn, which superstition says contains healing and magical powers as well as being an aphrodisiac and able to detect poison.

Enlightenment

Most of us humans tend to set up our lives like TV 'soap' operas and throw ourselves into the drama of our circumstances. All that pain, hurt, jealousy, anger or love is highly addictive and while we are involved in the play we feel alive, unhappy maybe, but definitely alive.

As you evolve you may decide to step aside and watch the drama in your life unfolding, without participating. You witness it, analysing your part and deciding how you can do it differently and with conscious awareness.

At this point a unicorn may appear in your life to help you take the next step, which is to move away from the scenario altogether and live life from another perspective.

The unicorn's horn from its third eye is a visible sign of enlightenment for unicorns are fully enlightened beings. They stand as a guide and an example.

With enlightenment consciousness you can be yourself—contented with your lot and able to see the divine in all.

So, if you are ready for this do not be surprised if you feel an invisible horse 'nudge' you, sense a unicorn near you or see one in your dreams. Then you may be aware of the light in all things and people, or just feel a sense of deep contentment.

Enlightenment just is. It is a state of being. It is acceptance. You cannot seek it for there is nothing to find. It is your essence and your birthright and many have attained different levels of it.

Some people have a moment of enlightenment or illumination, which is like switching on a light. Things may never be the same again for you see the divine in all things and people. Or it may fade. Either way nothing can take away that memory.

E X E R C I S E : Enlightenment Meditation

The aim of this meditation is to see the divine in all things, so that higher aspects of your third eye are being used.

Sometimes it is helpful to remember that the darkest hour is before the dawn and that it is the same with your consciousness. The more you feel you will never see, the nearer you are to bringing in the light. Of course, you can do this visualization as many times as you like.

1. Find a place where you can be quiet and undisturbed.
2. Ask the unicorns to place a cloak of Christ consciousness round you to protect you.
3. Sit comfortably and focus on your breathing. Be aware of the coolness in your nostrils as you breathe in and the relaxation of your spine as you breathe out. Repeat this ten times. Then breathe into your right knee ten times and out of your left one. Feel yourself relax more on each outbreath.
4. Ask your unicorn to come close and you may feel him nudge you or sense a tingle as he enters your aura.
5. Ask him to touch your third eye with his horn of light. Stay still for a little while after this.
6. Imagine your third eye as a huge ball in front of you. What is it like? What colour is it? How many doors or sections are still closed? How near to enlightenment are you?
7. Ask the unicorn to open one door. When he has done so, enter.
8. Who or what do you find here?
9. Let go of judgement. Simply bless whatever or whoever is there. See it from a much higher perspective and remember to ask your unicorn for guidance.
10. When you can truly find the divine message in the situation, that door in your third eye can remain open and you will carry more light.
11. Thank the unicorn.
12. Open your eyes.

CHAPTER 9

THE ROLES OF UNICORNS AND ANGELS

❁

Although both angels and unicorns belong to the angelic hierarchy, their roles are different. There is some overlap as they are beings of compassion and love and, because you have free will, if you want to have assistance from either of them, you must ask for it.

ᕙ

The Heart and the Soul

Unicorns work with you at a soul level. They help you fulfil your life purpose and bring joy and delight to your life. If you have great and noble ideals unicorns will be attracted to you, to enhance and empower your higher inspiration. Where your intention is pure but hope is beginning to dim, they will support and encourage you. If you are being derided for your forward thinking or aspirations they will uphold your dignity and strengthen your courage. If your light is pure and innocent, they will brighten and expand it.

If you desire to be a peacemaker, wish to help society or improve the lot of the sick, uneducated or impoverished, a unicorn will be drawn to you. It will open doors and strengthen you. If your soul longs for something, your unicorn will light you up and help make your wish come true.

A victim feels powerless and seeks someone to rescue and look after him. Unicorns will never work with victim consciousness for their task is to ennoble and encourage all aspiration. Of course, they will help someone in physical trouble if it is for their highest good. Guardian angels will answer the wishes of your heart. If you are in despair your angel will come to you to enfold and comfort you.

They will try to lift your spirits and help you find happiness. They are constantly looking for ways of bringing you love, if you are ready for it. They will ease your life by helping you find parking places, perfect presents or the right direction. You can also communicate with someone by asking your angel to talk to his or her angel and this can resolve many problems, which your personality may find difficult.

Your guardian angel holds the divine blueprint for your life and whispers in your ear. It constantly reminds you of better choices you can make, though you have free will to ignore such promptings. Many people have heard angels singing for they will sing over you to comfort you or raise your vibrations, often while you are asleep.

A Story

I met a doctor who had no truck with anything spiritual until he was introduced to a psychic at a friend's house. A few days later the son of another friend told him all about auras and added that he had always seen them. The doctor was astonished! That night he found my website and watched the TV clips, from which he learnt that everyone has a guardian angel, who will help you if you ask and it is easy to connect with it.

So he lay on his bed and asked for an angel to come to him. Immediately a deep blue light started to appear above him. Soon gold started to swirl in it. He watched with interest. Then the colours formed a vortex and began spinning down into his third eye. It felt extraordinary and he was sure it was an angelic presence. He asked the angels one question and it was unexpectedly answered that weekend.

He stayed with a different friend and heard wonderful cathedral music during the night. In the morning he asked his friend which CD she had played after he had gone to bed. Of course, she had been fast asleep and there was no music playing! Puzzled, he went into a bookshop and picked up my first angel book, *A Little Light on Angels*. It opened at the chapter "Angels Singing"!

He told me that the following day a baby stopped screaming the moment she was placed in his arms. The baby girl gazed into his eyes and he felt as if they were making a soul-to-soul connection, something he had never before experienced. That was only a beginning. From the day of the angelic intervention his patients, especially babies and children have all responded to him in a completely different way. He has become a spiritual healer and at the time of writing the unicorns are now waiting to work with him.

Guidance and Protection

Whenever I go on a car journey I thank the angels and unicorns for protecting and guiding my trip. I am often aware of several unicorns in front of the car, leading the way. The horses of light are always two or three feet above the ground. I cannot tell you what a wonderful feeling it gives me to have them guiding me. This does not always stop me from getting lost! However, I do assume that unicorn energy is needed in those places we 'accidentally' divert to.

Ask either the unicorn or angel kingdom for protection, guidance and direction in life. The more you talk to them and connect with them, the closer you will become to their energies and their wondrous qualities.

Healing

Both unicorns and angels give healing, for all beings of the seventh dimension can do so. Either can touch your chakras or spiritual energy centres, passing light into you. Or they can pour healing energy over you.

Rebecca had never worked with unicorns before. She had a painful leg and I suggested we call in the unicorns to point healing energy at her sore spot. We both had a sense of a beautiful unicorn coming in and she could feel something shifting in her leg. The pain disappeared completely. They literally pour high-frequency light out of their horns and this dissolves the blockage or karma, which creates the pain.

Saving You from Death or Danger

When does a unicorn save you and when an angel? If it is not your time to die or your karma to suffer it is the role of your guardian angel to step in and save you. However, your unicorn may also assist you. Just like angels a unicorn will sometimes respond to a call for help out of pure compassion. At others the person may have a close though unconscious connection with his unicorn.

A man once told me that when he thought he was drowning, he was held up by a white horse until help arrived. So, I was interested to learn that the white foam on the sea is called white horses because sailors of old saw unicorns holding above the waves the heads of their mates who would otherwise have drowned

When Kathy Crosswell and I were looking at hundreds of photographs containing orbs for our books, *Enlightenment Through Orbs* and *Ascension Through Orbs*, we were presented with several series of pictures taken at one-minute intervals or less. In one of these unicorn and fairy orbs were travelling together, in a violent storm, on the ocean in order to help people on boats and sea creatures.

Because the power of a storm can sometimes impel certain individuals to throw themselves into the waters, the unicorns were also patrolling to save anyone with such a compulsion.

Blessings

You can ask both unicorns and angels to bless people, places and situations through you. The information is in the chapter on Unicorn Blessings.

EXERCISE: Heart and Soul

1. Take two sheets of paper. Write at the top of the first one, "Things that make my heart sing," and on the second, "Things that satisfy my soul."
2. List on the first page things that you have or that you wish for that make you happy. These may include a good job, romantic relationship, success at a task, and even a new car.
3. List on the second page whatever makes you feel deeply contented, connected to the divine and satisfied. Some of these may include open hearted service, creative, artistic or musical expression, deep meditation, being in nature, even to have a child, if that is your soul longing.

EXERCISE: Visualization

1. Find a place where you can be quiet and undisturbed.
2. If possible prepare your space by playing soft music, lighting a candle or joss stick, creating an altar or finding a few flowers to raise the energy.

3. Close your eyes and be aware of your eyelids becoming heavy. Focus on your toes on the outbreath and feel them relax. Then continue through your body, relaxing your feet, ankles, calves, knees, thighs, abdomen, lower back, spine, back of your neck, chest, arms, hands, shoulders, face and scalp.

4. Ask Archangel Gabriel to place a pure white bubble of protection all round you.

5. Imagine yourself in a woodland glade. You may be able to smell the moist grass and flowers, hear the trickle of a stream or feel the soft sun on your face.

6. Your guardian angel is walking towards you across the clearing. With it is a magnificent pure white unicorn. They are coming right up to you.

7. Tell your guardian angel about the wishes of your heart and ask for help and guidance about lighting up your life with these things. Listen for a reply.

8. Tell your unicorn about the longings of your soul and listen for a response.

9. Your guardian angel is placing her hands on your heart at the front and back. You may feel her love flow in as she opens you up to receive your heart's desire.

10. Your unicorn is touching your third eye with the light from its horn. Again you may be aware of the sensation as more of your soul energy is brought into you.

11. Your angel and unicorn are enfolding you in a beautiful soft pink light, helping you to integrate the higher energies.

12. Thank them and open your eyes.

CHAPTER 10

UNICORNS AND CHILDREN

Babies and children are open to spirit and especially to fairies and unicorns. This is why so many children's toys are decorated with unicorns as well as playful fairies. I have heard of many children's unicorn parties but here is a story about a unicorn cake.

A Unicorn Cake

Margi had moved into her new house on a complex in Johannesburg. The builder was big and burly, the most unlikely person to know about unicorns, or so she thought. One day he said he wanted to show Margi something, which was in the house next door. She followed him to the neighbouring house and there in the kitchen was a unicorn cake, which he had made for his granddaughter's birthday. It was surrounded with unicorns and he had little unicorns made in sugar for each child at the party. He said to Margi: "Do you think she'll like it?"

Margi said, "No!", and his face fell. When Margi added, "She won't like it. She'll love it!", the big man beamed. "Do you really think so?', he exclaimed in delight.

On Monday morning she saw him and asked how the party went. "It was fantastic. She absolutely adored it and the children all loved their sugar unicorns. It was unbelievably successful!"

Pre-birth Supervision

Now that there are so many indigo, rainbow, sun and crystal children being born who are the enlightened ones carrying a very high frequency, unicorns are connecting with them and teaching them before birth. Their spirits gather in a small group of six or seven for instruction in the inner planes. Occasionally they teach a large class.

The unicorns have always connected pre-birth with those who have a special mission to further the progress of humanity in some way. They implant a star in their aura, so that when the individual enters the cloudy negativity of Earth their light can be pinpointed. The angels and unicorns make a special effort to locate and assist these children.

They place five-pointed stars in the auras of those souls who are striving to perfect themselves, so that they can, through their own growth, help others. They place six-pointed ones in the auras of those with a vision to bring heaven to earth.

A few, who have been specially trained, are distinguished with a seven-pointed star, so that they can lead an ascension team.

Another reason for the close pre-birth supervision and education of the enlightened children from Orion is that so many of them cannot cope with the heavy vibrations of Earth. On occasions part of their soul withdraws resulting in what doctors call autism or autistic tendencies. Unicorn energy can help them stay grounded in our reality.

Riding Horses

I know a little girl who lives on the edge. She is excitable, sometimes withdrawn and can be quite challenging to handle.

Her mother enrolled her in a ballet class with her friends but the child refused to join in. The little girl explained that while she loved the Angelina Ballerina stories and reading about ballet she did not want to do it. So her mother tried swimming lessons. No, she was not interested. Gymnastics was boring. Then her mother offered the child a horse-riding lesson and she was enthusiastic.

Apparently, at the first lesson the little girl sat on the horse for half an hour while the trainer led the animal round. She went into a state of blissful trance and did not want to dismount. The mood lasted long after they had gone home. And each week it was the same. Just being in contact with the horse took her into another space where she found peace and stillness.

I believe this special child was able to make connection with unicorn energy while she was on the horse and this enabled her to feel safe and belonging. It was her time of spiritual connection.

Children See Unicorns

Flavia-Kate, who works with the unicorns, wrote: "It was children who first noticed the unicorns around me. I give talks to groups and often people bring their children along. Children can be quite spiritually-sighted and it was often a joy when some ran up to me at the end of a session and shouted, with excitement, 'We can see your unicorns!'"

Taking Children to the Unicorn Kingdom

Sometimes, as I lie in bed preparing for sleep, I visualize myself taking my grandchildren who are two and five at the time of writing to a beautiful sacred garden, where we meet unicorns. Then we ride on their backs and they take us to the unicorn kingdom.

At first we rode together on one huge unicorn then gradually they started to ride their own little unicorns. Once in the seventh heaven they play with the great creatures and receive pure energy, healing and tuition. I believe that at some level their spirits are with me and it feels like a gift of love to take them with me.

EXERCISE: Light a Candle

Light a candle each morning and ask unicorns to go to specific children. You do not necessarily need to know them but your active thoughts create a bridge of light that makes it easier for the unicorns to connect with some of them.

CHAPTER 11

THE UNICORN SENSES

Unicorns are like finely tuned instruments. They have a highly evolved sense of smell. Like humans they love the perfume of happiness and are repelled by the stench of anger. Of course, they don't eat, as they have no physical body to nourish, so they don't taste.

Hearing

As higher-frequency-creatures unicorns can hear notes and tones that are out of our auditory range. Often they listen to the music beyond the sounds we hear.

They can pick out much higher frequencies and hundreds of notes that we simply miss. Every living thing sends out music, whether it is grass growing, the sun rising or a planet moving. Your aura too plays musical notes, the quality of which depends on the state of your consciousness. Your unicorn can hear it all.

Like all highly evolved beings, the unicorns love beautiful harmony. Human voice has always had the power to heal and uplift. For example, if someone has a singing voice so glorious that it can raise the consciousness of those who listen, the unicorns will be at the concert watching the energies and adding their own light. Or if the timbre of your voice is on an angelic or healing vibration, they will work with you.

They listen to the music of the spheres, the melody of running water, the sigh of the wind and the angels singing. For example, a beautiful garden, full of flowers and an emerald lawn, with a fountain, emanates wonderful musical notes. To a unicorn it sounds like an orchestra playing a beautiful symphony. They also love wild gardens where elementals play. A neglected garden with a stagnant pond or piles of rubbish sounds to them like heavy metal! They move away fast.

They find the hum of an electricity substation very disturbing. Quarrelling, screaming or any form of discord is distasteful and they withdraw. This also applies to those emotions, whether in acting or reality, which emit from TV or radio.

Hammering, drilling or a noisy engine radiate vibrations like the heat of a furnace, from which the unicorns pull away as quickly as you would if you were being singed by a fire.

Emotions have a sound and a smell. Anger sounds like barking, while passive anger yaps or growls. Even a sullen person has a growling, keep away from me aura! We may sense it but a unicorn hears it. Love, compassion and joy sound like beautiful melodious music, contentment gently purrs, while higher aspiration sends out thrilling clarion calls.

Of course, your unicorn's pure and glorious aura plays the most extraordinary tunes and harmonics, well beyond your auditory range. It is so wonderful that it tunes up everything around it to a higher octave. The sounds they emit can touch people profoundly, to the very depth of their souls.

At one time all villagers would attend their local church on Sundays and as they sang hymns, they would automatically come into harmony for the highest purpose of the local community. Those who were emotionally or mentally out of alignment would be re-tuned by the voices of their friends and by the angels who would sing with them. In this way neighbours could live in peace.

Unicorns also hear and respond to the intention and energy of sound, so where there is beautiful music, sacred chanting or choirs singing in harmony together the unicorns will add their light. The sound of a mother crooning to her baby will draw a unicorn to pour love over the two of them.

And they are attracted to joyful laughter, inspirational conversation, loving words and the chatter of children playing happily. A cat purring, a bird pouring out its heart in song, the breeze in the trees or waves lapping onto a shore is music to a unicorn. Melodious wind chimes call them in.

Sight

Humans are discovering that as they raise their vibrations, they can see subtle shades that they could not before. And more and more people are opening up to enlightenment and developing their psychic vision, clairvoyance and claircogniscence. Unicorns are totally enlightened, all knowing, all seeing beings, so they can see a spectrum way beyond our visual range. They can see both with their physical eyes and their third eye.

Smell

Unicorns have a fine and delicate sense of smell. All your thoughts have an aroma. We talk of the smell of fear. It is sharp. Anger is acrid like burning or explosive, while passive anger is more like a bad drain. Jealousy is like ammonia. If your thoughts and emotions stink, then no matter how you justify yourself, unicorns will avoid you. On the other hand if you are full of love, contentment, peace and noble thoughts, your aura is beautifully perfumed.

Love is like a fragrant rose; compassion a lily; a warm, nourishing and open heart literally enfolds people in the smell of baking, at such a subtle level they cannot physically discern it—but the unicorns can.

EXERCISE: Unicorn Sound

Here is an exercise which I have done in a variety of ways in different places and which always brings in the unicorns. They love it. It helps to harmonize a group and can produce profound feelings of serenity.

You will need a group of people who divide into two, three or four groups, though it is possible to do with two or three people only.

1. Each group finds a quiet space.
2. Together they create a sound, tune, tone or chant dedicated to the unicorns. This usually takes ten minutes or more.
3. When they are ready they return to the main space and each group in turn offers their unicorn music.
4. One group starts and after a minute or two, the second group comes in with their music and harmonizes with the first one.
5. Then the third group enters, again harmonizing to create something greater than their individual song.

6. The fourth group enters.
7. The harmony continues until a group is ready to stop and each one withdraws gently.
8. All sit quietly tuning in to the sound and the presence of the unicorns.

EXERCISE: Unicorn Sound and Movement

This is the same exercise but each group adds a flowing movement. When they join together, they harmonize the movement and the sound.

EXERCISE: Unicorn Sound, Colour and Movement

The groups act as above but each chooses a colour that they visualize. Psychically the colours will be seen to swirl and merge around the people as they move and sing or tone.

CHAPTER 12

UNICORN WISHES

Ancient myths tell us that unicorns grant wishes to the pure of heart. This really means that they open doors for those who are truly ready to receive with gratitude, joy and integrity.

When a pure innocent child makes a wish from the bottom of his heart, a unicorn will draw close to the little one, to help him. If the wish is for his highest good, the unicorn will bring it about. However, like all things on this planet it is subject to spiritual law. If a bereaved child desperately wishes for his mother to come back, the unicorn cannot make her live again. This is a soul level decision made by the mother and all concerned before incarnation and no being of light can countermand such a commitment. However, the unicorn can bring someone with motherly energy to comfort and help the child.

Many children as well as adults feel depressed, confused and lonely, their lives tinged with grey. If asked, the unicorns can help to return the sparkle and magic to them.

Spiritual Laws

The Law of Prayer is, "Ask, believe and it is already granted." In other words, the Universe responds to faith.

The Law of Manifestation says that when you focus on your vision without doubt or deviation, it must be granted. The first step is clarity. It is vitally important that you decide what you really want before you ask for it. Indecision sends out a confused energy, so that the unicorns cannot help you. When you are clear what you really want to aim for, focus on it. Imagine you already have it. Then tell the unicorns what you want. Be careful how you word this.

If, for example, you say that you will do anything to help AIDS orphans, you may find your life changes dramatically and that you are overwhelmed with opportunities beyond your capacity. Words have power. It is more prudent to say: "I offer myself in service to AIDS orphans and am open to guidance." If your intention is pure and clear your life will change in a way that you can manage.

Clarity

EXERCISE: Getting Clarity

1. Write down your wish.
2. Draw it as if it has happened.
3. Colour round it the shades of feeling it brings to you.
4. Does this feel completely right to you? If yes, check it out with the Clarity meditation below. If not, think again.

EXERCISE: Clarity Meditation

1. Close your eyes, imagine you are sitting in a magic toadstool circle.
2. Your unicorn comes to you and you tell it what you wish for.
3. Climb onto his back and he moves gently into the inner worlds with you.
4. Approach a door marked with your name.
5. When you knock on the door it opens and you enter a world where your wish is reality.
6. Take time to experience it. Here you can change anything.
7. How does your body feel? Do you feel light and happy?
8. When you are certain you have it right you can ask the unicorn to bring you back.

EXERCISE: Unicorn Wish Meditation

1. Find somewhere that you can be relaxed and undisturbed.
2. Close your eyes and let go of the outside world.
3. Let your guardian angel sit by you with one wing round you.
4. Visualize a sparkling white stairway stretching ahead of you.
5. A beautiful rainbow light cascades down the steps.
6. Through the misty rainbow a glorious unicorn appears, walking down the steps towards you. He greets you and invites you to climb onto his back.
7. Your angel lifts you on to the unicorn and sits behind you, his wings enfolding you.

8. The unicorn turns and climbs the steps. You can see the rainbow mist swirling round your legs.
9. You emerge into sunlight and ahead there is a great arch with beautifully scented roses growing all over it. The unicorn takes you through it.
10. On the other side there is a soft green glade full of wild flowers and an ancient wishing well in the centre.
11. Your angel helps you down from your unicorn.
12. You pick up a pebble from the ground. Hold it carefully, bless it and make your wish into it.
13. Ask the unicorn to bless your wish by touching the pebble with his horn.
14. Drop the pebble with your wish in it into the well. Listen for the splash.
15. One droplet of water comes back to the surface. Catch it and hand it to the unicorn with gratitude.
16. Sit on the moss and visualize your life as if the wish has already been granted.
17. Your angel helps you once more onto his back and you return through the arch of roses, down the rainbow steps to where you started.
18. Thank the angel and your unicorn.

Unicorn Wish Games and Exercises

EXERCISE: Unicorn Wish Spiral 1

1. A spiral is a sacred shape. When you draw or trace one in a clockwise direction you bring in sacred energy to energize your wish.
2. When the direction is anti-clockwise you pull out any negative energy that has been blocking you, so that your wish can manifest. This exercise helps to open your third eye.
3. Draw a big spiral and place a unicorn in the middle of it. This is not a test of artistic ability. You can draw the unicorn yourself or trace one, then cut it out and glue it or use a silver star to symbolize it.
4. Each person in turn traces their spiral with their finger and when they reach the unicorn at the centre, they make a wish.

EXERCISE: Unicorn Wish Spiral 2

You can if you want to mark out a spiral with chalk, pebbles, shells, twigs or anything you wish to. Then you can walk round it, making a wish when you reach the centre.

EXERCISE: Unicorn Labyrinth Wish

The labyrinth is a more complex and powerful symbol than the spiral. As you trace or walk this shape you are symbolically travelling the sacred journey of your life: going into the heart of your being, then returning out into the world again.

This exercise helps to harmonize the right and left brain, as both sides of your brains are computers, which can then work together more easily. It enables your unicorn to bring about your wish more readily.

1. Draw a labyrinth and place a unicorn or something to represent one in the centre. You can also use the one below.
2. Trace the labyrinth with your finger.
3. Pause when you reach the unicorn in the centre and make a wish.
4. Again trace the journey out with your finger.

There are full instructions on how to draw your own labyrinth in my book *Discover Atlantis: A Guide to Reclaiming the Wisdom of the Ancients.*

EXERCISE: Unicorn Wish on a Star

This too is a very powerful way of manifesting wishes. You can do it with two or more people, so be careful what you wish for.

1. Cut out a silver star for each person, or each hold a small crystal.
2. One person (A) shares their wish with the others—something that fills them with joy.
3. (A) then holds the star or crystal between their palms.
4. The others each place their palms around (A).
5. (A) states their wish aloud.
6. Together they invoke the unicorns and ask them to make this wish come true.
7. Everyone focuses on the wish and imagine that it has already been granted.
8. Share your impressions.
9. Then the other participants take their turn.

EXERCISE: Making a Unicorn Wishing Well

1. Decorate a plate or bowl with flowers to represent your wishing well. You can, of course, use your creative imagination.
2. You may like to play unicorn music, for example Andrew Brel's Angel and Unicorns music.
3. Write a wish for yourself on a piece of paper.
4. With integrity you can write a wish for someone else.
5. Hold hands, if there are two or more of you, and say: "Beloved Unicorns, we ask you to take these wishes from our hearts and bring them into reality. Thank you."

CHAPTER 13

THE UNICORN KINGDOM

Horses come from Lakumay, which is an ascended star near the constellation of Sirius and is beyond the frequency we can see. In the higher planes around Lakumay are found the unicorn kingdoms. Imagine a place where it is light, beautiful and harmonious. Here in soft green-blue meadows, rich with flowers and aglow with colour the light-hearted unicorns love to gallop and frolic. Even the trees radiate light and the ascended horses are found browsing amongst them, enjoying the beauty of nature. Here butterflies the size of small birds flutter from flower to flower or spread their wings and bask in the atmosphere.

Other creatures whose home planet is Sirius visit this wonderful plane. Birds come from Sirius and some visit Lakumay for spiritual growth and teachings. They do not have the same colours as they do on Earth. Drab little sparrows become a cheerful orange and flocks of them twitter happily together or dare to fly near the magnificent unicorns. Shy modest little wrens are pale pink. Peacocks are clothed in regal blues. Amongst them are pure white birds, individual or in small clusters, who have mastered their lessons and ascended to a higher frequency.

Dolphins too come from Sirius. When they incarnate they hold for Earth the wisdom of all time. Their minds are like huge advanced computers, so they keep the history of all that has happened here. Twelve species of dolphins each hold a segment of information and knowledge, which is why it is a tragedy and disaster when humans decimate a variety. They telepathically impart selected information to people who are ready to understand it and this is one of the ways that our divine inheritance is being returned to us.

Dolphins and unicorns have a very close relationship, not only because they have the same planet of origin, but because they can communicate and exchange information. They can also interact through play. No being is too evolved to enjoy pure fun.

All fish originate from Sirius and come to experience life in the waters of Earth. Their service work is to keep the oceans clean but some species protect the angel dolphins that hold the profound wisdom and knowledge of Atlantis. Others have different tasks, ecological and social. Some are simply here to enjoy and learn.

They all communicate with and learn from their elder brethren, the unicorns in the inner planes, just as we are privileged to do.

Music

In the unicorn kingdom you can hear the Seraphim singing, the music of the spheres, the grass growing and the birds singing. It is just as Earth but at a higher frequency. To a human it might sound silent, as our hearing is not attuned to such a vibration.

Do Unicorns Maintain Their Horse Shape When in Their Own Kingdom?

As seventh-dimensional beings they can assume any shape and do so if this is needed. They would not choose to take a human form however, though an angel may do so.

They love and respect the shape that Source created for them. It gives them balance and enormous strength. A human may envy and admire a horse galloping with its mane and tail blowing in the breeze. In their own kingdom in the inner planes they can run in the same way and enjoy their essence of freedom.

Their kingdom is magnificent. With our limited vision we may perceive it to be pure white but unicorns can see all the shades of the rainbow within the white and many more than we have any idea of. We are blessed that they have once more come to Earth to help us. At the same time we can recognize that we have earned the right to their assistance. Under the spiritual Laws of Attraction thousands of people have radiated enough light to draw the unicorns to this planet again.

The following are just a few of the ways people have been raising the energy of the planet. Monks and nuns chanting sacred words send out a huge light into the Universe. A hermit focussed on prayer can mitigate great clouds of karma. Individuals sitting in meditation, choirs singing hymns and people reading spiritual books, all emit light, which adds to the collective pool of higher energy.

Of course everyone can add to the pool of light. Every single thought you send out is repellent or magnetic to creatures of light. If you live in a concrete jungle, drink excessively, swear, gossip, curse others and are greedy or selfish, your aura will repel these pure beings of light.

EXERCISE: Becoming Closer to the Unicorn Kingdom

1. Develop the qualities of love, peace, dignity, hope, joy and integrity. These give your aura a pure clear glow, which is magnetic to people and unicorns. You can do this by making conscious choices to change your attitude.
2. Help other people from a genuine desire to serve.
3. Ask to meet unicorns in your dreams. I explain how you can do this in Chapter 17, "Working with Unicorn Dreams".
4. Think about them, read about them, talk about them, draw them—in other words focus your attention on unicorns.
5. Take quiet time each day to call in unicorn blessings and guidance.
6. Imagine yourself with them. Visualize yourself walking or riding with them.
7. Walk or simply be in nature.

Visiting the Unicorn Kingdom

The seventh heaven contains the angelic kingdom and the unicorn kingdom. When your light is bright enough, you can visit either of these during meditation or dreams. If you are reading this book, assume you are ready and the portals of this realm will open to you. You must ask, of course, and most people do this unconsciously. Your thoughts are invitations to everything that comes into your life.

If a unicorn takes you to their kingdom you may be surprised at other invitees you meet there, where their personality and ego has been stripped away. We can never judge others for those we consider unworthy may be very different at a soul level. That grumpy, disagreeable man you never liked may have a spark of pure gold in his soul and you may see him in the unicorn kingdom with a pink and purple aura, a radiant smile and eyes filled with love.

Of course there are some people you will never meet in the unicorn kingdom because their soul energy is not high enough to reach this sphere.

Walk in the Unicorn Kingdom

One evening a friend of mine called round, as she wanted to work with her vision of her future. We had a great time and got clarity about her goals.

When Mother Mary asked me to write this unicorn book, I protested that I didn't have enough information. She told me to set aside a week for living with them. I was not quite sure how I was supposed to manage this in my busy schedule but decided to do what I could.

Next morning I went for a walk. Setting off to my local woods I let the unicorns take me rather than treading my usual path. They led me off the main way through some trees to a clearing, where there was a knoll of five trees on the far side. I knew someone to whom Archangel Michael had appeared at this spot, so I occasionally came here to soak in the energy. Sadly when the forest was being thinned out, very much to our shock, one of the five trees was felled. However, it is still there in its etheric form and I sometimes go there to bless it and receive blessings from it.

The unicorns intimated that I must be aware of my feet on the earth as well as the trees and everything around me. At the same time I was to take part of my consciousness to the unicorn kingdom. What happened was extraordinary and beautiful. A wonderful feeling of peace came over me as I sensed unicorns around me.

Ordinary birds became balls of beautiful light and colour. A friendly robin glowed turquoise. To my surprise, blackbirds shimmered white. I asked, "Are all blackbirds white here?" The reply came, "No!" I was shown some who were radiating a gentle lilac shade.

The unicorns intimated that I was to look down at the trees on Earth. One said, "You humans see their auras as a band of white sparkling light round them. We see shafts of gold reaching up to the heavens as they transmit their wisdom into the etheric. Remember trees are the keepers of wisdom of the land. Honour them. Many of them are venerable beings. Many have much more evolved under-standing than humans. They have different experiences from you. They witness, absorb and learn. They feel energies. They shelter and protect. Sometimes a person can even become invisible when in the protection of a very wise tree elemental."

"Really!" I thought.

There was magic in the woods that day as I walked in a blissful state of contemplative awareness, spanning the dimensions. I became aware that more and more birds surrounded me. A chaffinch hopped along in front of me; sparrows darted here and there; a robin, a thrush, and several wood pigeons all flew close as if to say 'hello'. I felt they were acknowledging the energy of the Unicorn kingdom.

Then I reached the road at the end of the forest and the wonder was over.

EXERCISE: So How Can You Take a Unicorn Walk?

First make sure you are somewhere congenial to unicorns. It would be very difficult for them to reach you in the middle of a concrete jungle—not impossible, but harder. Try to find somewhere green; woods, meadows or even a park.

1. Be grounded, so be conscious of the earth beneath your feet and all that surrounds you in your physical third-dimensional reality.
2. Feel something tangible. It may be a fir cone, the bark of a tree, a pebble or a blade of grass.
3. Notice the smells and perfumes around you.
4. Then become aware of your breathing and let it be full and natural.
5. Take your consciousness to the unicorn kingdom. You can do this by imagining you are very tall and there are unicorns moving around you at the higher levels. Or project your mind into the land of the ascended horses and sense what is going on there. Talk to them, listen and enjoy what you are experiencing.
6. When your walk is over make sure you are fully back in your physical body. You can do this by walking very consciously or by touching something.
7. Only do this walk where you are safe and never where there is traffic! Above all enjoy it.

CHAPTER 14

Unicorn Blessings

W hen you bring divine energy through your heart and offer it to someone or something, you bless them. You bless them by offering them something they lack or believe they lack. If they open up to receive it, your blessing, for an instant, can bring them into divine wholeness.

If someone feels they lack money, bless them with prosperity. If their relationship is collapsing, bless them in perfect love. If they are sad, lonely, angry or feel a failure, bless them with happiness, friendship, peace and success. There is a divine abundance of all these qualities. Remember that everything you send out comes back to you, enriching you beyond measure.

By asking the unicorns to bless through you, the recipient also receives their ineffable energy and light.

Receiving Unicorn Blessings

Unicorn blessings are profound and powerful. When you receive them, your body often feels tingly as the pure energy comes through you. You can invoke one directly or someone else may send you one. Either way, the more receptive you are the better. If you do not know that someone is sending you a unicorn blessing and are unprepared, the beings of light will ensure that their energy flows into you very gently. You will receive it!

Angel and Unicorn Blessings

You can ask both unicorns and angels to bless people, places and situations through you. If you want to call in the angels, raise your hands in the air, ask the angels to touch them and while they do this imagine them becoming golden. Then from your golden hands you can send angelic blessings or healing to wherever it is needed. Of course, you can simply mentally send an angel blessing.

Sending Unicorn Blessings

If you are working with unicorns, raise your hands in the air and ask the unicorns to touch them. Sense them sparkling with pure white light. You may even feel them tingling or see silver white stars shimmering from your fingers. Alternatively you can mentally send out unicorn blessings to where they are needed. You can also physically place your unicorn healing hands on someone but ask for permission first.

For example, you can send out unicorn blessings to everyone with whom you come into contact during the day. In stationary traffic bless all the motorists with patience and peace. Raise your hand, so that the unicorn stars and stream of energy go out to touch everyone concerned. In fast moving traffic send the blessings from your third eye and let the unicorn energy influence everyone to drive safely.

You can be an immense force for good by working with these extraordinary beings of light. This list may help you to differentiate when to send angel blessings and when to send unicorn ones. Sometimes the angels or unicorns will accompany the blessing and be there to help.

Unicorn Blessings

Beings of light like the unicorns only see high qualities, such as love, honesty, serenity and joy. They simply do not recognize that anything lower exists, which is why they must withdraw from negativity. Therefore they bring out characteristics such as purity, truth and courage. Their blessings bring out the goodness that is available in all beings on Earth.

No one ever needs to feel useless, for even if you are unemployed, housebound, disabled, or sick you can add to the pool of blessings in the world. Blessing with unicorn energy can transform you into a pure light.

Remember that when you invoke a blessing, you are calling forward divine unicorn energy to touch the person, situation, or place. A blessing is as powerful as your intention and can heal feelings and situations.

Education Establishments

If you pass a school or college, bless the teachers for their dedication, their integrity and ability to light up the hearts and minds of their charges. Bless the pupils in their interest and their ability to learn, concentrate and achieve to the best of their ability. Imagine the building being flooded in white light and each person in it walking tall with bright eyes and happy expressions.

Food

While you are preparing food bless it. Thank the vegetables as you chop them. If you crack an egg, think of the hen laying it and send it a blessing. Before you eat hold your hands over your food and ask the unicorns for a blessing. They will send it through your heart and out of your hands. You can also ask the angels and unicorns to bless your food together. Then you will receive both unicorn and angelic energies in your food, which will ultimately light up the cells of your body.

Water

I was talking to Marjut in Finland, who told me that the unicorns had impressed on her that they were very happy to bless our water before we drink it. Since then I have held up my cup or glass and asked the unicorns to bless the contents. I can picture one of them showering stars into it from its horn and I am certain the water tastes lighter and sweeter. Furthermore I know that the subtle energy of the liquid is much higher than it was before.

Remember to bless the rain in its cleansing, healing and nourishment. When I pass puddles I hold out my hand and ask the unicorns to send their blessings through it into the water.

People

Call on the unicorns to bless a person and you can be sure, one of the luminous creatures will approach that individual and gently touch them with its horn of light. When you call forth a blessing on a number of people together the unicorns gather above them and shower them in symbols of hope and love.

Politicians and Business People

Bless politicians and business people in their honour, integrity, wisdom and ability to make decisions that will benefit and empower everyone.

The Media

Television and Radio

When you watch television or listen to the radio call on the unicorn energy and feel it flowing through you. Then bless the programmes and the people in them.

Bless the potential not the reality as you see it. This means you can bless the 'soap' and low-frequency programmes in their spreading of love, kindness, friendliness, wisdom, empathy and justice. Your blessing will enable the tiniest threads of these qualities to grow and develop.

Newspapers and Magazines

I asked if the unicorns could help lighten up the newspapers and magazines that seem focussed on the negative side of life. The unicorns agreed that most of the media outlets were putting their attention on the darkness. They added that this was currently part of the divine plan because all secrets and hidden corners must be revealed. The time for that is now. Spin seeks to obscure the truth. It is the reaction of the dark forces to the probing of the light. It too will pass.

The media does, however, have things out of balance. There is too much depression and not enough inspiration.

What You Can Do to Help

First ask the unicorns to communicate with editors, programme producers and people of influence in the media. Direct them to whisper into the ears of those who are ready to listen to suggestions of inspiration, to praise the newsworthiness of courage, service, and happiness. If you do this regularly you become a spiritual link between the media and the unicorns.

Through the rainbow bridge of light you create, some of those with influence will hear and respond.

You can ask the unicorns to work with editors of papers, programmes and magazines that are ready to feature the positive, the hopeful and the good. Then the unicorns can strengthen them to stand up for integrity, justice and light.

There are also magazines and papers dedicated to the positive: in the UK, for example, there is a magazine called *Positive News*. Cygnus Books sends out a quarterly magazine full of inspiration and spiritual information, the *Cygnus Review*.

Ask the unicorns to bless and encourage the editors who spread these good tidings.

Children and Teenagers

Bless all children and teenagers with innocence, happiness, and zest for life. Do this especially for those who have lost their way.

Parents

Bless mothers with love, nurturing, patience, and the joy of mothering. Bless fathers with love, fairness, and fathering skills.

Animals

Bless animals with love, harmlessness, and a joyous acceptance of life. You may want to bless some of them with the capacity for forgiveness or courage.

Nature

Bless trees in their wisdom, strength, and healing powers.

Those of Lower Consciousness

Bless thieves, cheats or liars in the abundance and honesty that lies within them. Bless violent thugs and terrorists with peace, self-worth, confidence, and serenity. Bless malingerers with a sense of worth and feeling of belonging.

Computers and Technology

Bless all the modern technological goods that you use, so you will not turn them into technological bads. Remember, crystal chips have a consciousness, which responds to your thoughts and attitudes. Send love and blessings to them all. Bring the purity and light of the unicorns into them and they will reward you with a longer life and trouble-free use.

Places and Situations

Bless all places and situations in their divine perfection and with all the qualities you wish to endow on them. If you bless a country with peace, the energy of peace will be divinely guided to where it is needed in this country. Bless the divine essence hidden in all things and people. And remember to thank the unicorns for blessing others through you.

All blessings help in some way. You may only receive thanks or feedback from a few individuals but know you are adding to the accumulation of good in the world.

EXERCISE: A Blessing Walk

This is a very simple thing to do whenever you take a walk. You need to be very alert so that you see and bless all things and creatures on your way. You can do this mentally as you walk along or by holding out your hands and directing unicorn blessings towards the items on which you are focussing.

1. Thank the unicorns for protecting and blessing the home or other place that you have left.
2. Ask them to accompany you and bless your walk.
3. Ask them to bless the weather, whether it is rain, snow, sun or wind.
4. Bless the trees, the flowers, the grass and anything growing.
5. Bless the people and animals you pass.
6. Bless the insects you see and even those hidden from your eyes.
7. Bless the earth beneath your feet.
8. Bless the pebbles and stones.
9. Bless any cars, trains or aeroplanes you see or hear.
10. Notice how you feel when you finish.

You can if you wish do a unicorn blessing while on a car journey, doing housework or gardening or performing any other task that leaves part of your mind free to do so.

Each time you do this it will add light to all around you and also increase your own light quotient.

CHAPTER 15

HEALING RELATIONSHIPS

You can ask your angel to talk to someone else's angel to help resolve any misunderstandings and conflicts. They will help both parties in their intervention.

Unicorn energy is different. You must be willing to set aside the claims of your ego, of being 'right' or wanting to hold onto hurt or anger. Then, if you have a sincere wish for the highest outcome in a relationship, your unicorn will assist.

Prayer of Surrender

Start with a prayer to help you let go of your ego attachments within the relationship. What blocks you from seeing the divine in the other person? Is it your desire to be right or treated as important? Are you tenaciously clinging onto feeling hurt, angry, envious, and if so, why? Does it make you feel superior or inferior? Does it justify your behaviour? Are you ready to let go of your attachment to envy, jealousy or being loved, successful, wronged or feeling unhappy?

You may need to surrender a whole list of things. Remember that you have attracted this individual, group or situation to your patterns. At a soul level you have decided to learn this lesson, so they are your teacher.

Prayer

"I am now willing to let go of my attachment to _____ .
I surrender. I recognize you, _____ (name),
as my great teacher. We are one. I call on the unicorns to open my heart and mind towards you to bring about harmony between us. So be it. It is done."

Unicorn Healing Rainbow

This is a visualization to take a healing rainbow from your heart to the other person's. Now, of course, they have free will and neither you nor your unicorn can make them open their heart to you. They may have other agendas, which may result in them refusing your offer. However, if you have genuinely surrendered, the other person will feel the shift in your energy and will usually open their heart to receive the other end of the rainbow. Then you can allow peace, love, abundance or whatever is needed to flow between you.

As with any exercise like the healing rainbow below, you may have to do the visualization several times before you notice a difference in your relationship. One day you may feel you would like to telephone or write to them. Or you may be content that the situation between you is resolved and be happy not to approach the other.

When the unicorns gave me the healing rainbow visualization I immediately thought of a friend with whom I did not see eye to eye. We were now on less than happy terms. I sat down and asked the unicorns to touch my heart and help me clear all negativity from the relationship. Interestingly I bumped into this friend a couple of days later and he immediately came up to me and asked for a hug. The unicorns helped again!

Remember you can do this even if the other person has passed over. This is sometimes much easier than when they are in a physical body and they will be ready to open their heart to you from the higher perspective they have on the other side.

EXERCISE: Healing Rainbow Visualization

1. Sit quietly where you will be undisturbed.
2. Breathe comfortably in and out of your heart centre until you feel relaxed.
3. Ask your unicorn to touch your heart with his horn. Trust that this has happened or visualize this happening.
4. Imagine your heart is a rose and sense the petals opening wide.
5. Picture the other person sitting some distance from you.
6. Imagine your unicorn taking a rainbow from your heart to the other person's.
7. Send love and any other qualities you feel inspired to bestow along the rainbow.

8. When you feel ready you can send a message from your heart to theirs.
9. After a little while sense how your heart feels.
10. You may have received impressions or even a message from the other person.
11. Thank the other person and your unicorn. Then put a rainbow cloak over your aura and open your eyes.

Healing between Bullies and Victims

Bullies and victims have the same fear. It is just expressed differently. The bully wants to be loved and respected but does not believe he deserves it, so he throws his weight about to make himself feel better or more important. The victim wants to be loved and respected but is afraid he is helpless and not good enough. His fear attracts a bully in.

The bully needs to surrender the feeling that he is powerless to get the love and respect he craves and be prepared to acknowledge his own worth. The victim needs to surrender fear and lack of worth and be prepared to step into his power by claiming his courage and self-respect.

Bully-victim situations sometimes arise between husband and wife, siblings, bosses and their workers, colleagues or companies. It occurs wherever there is fear. It does not matter whether the bully or the victim is ready to let go first and make peace. If this applies to you, do the unicorn healing rainbow and your unicorn will assist you.

And if you observe the bully-victim-dance taking place between two people you know, call in the unicorns, open your heart and create a healing rainbow from your heart to both of theirs.

Healing between Countries, Organizations and Religions

There are countless examples of countries bullying weaker ones. Most rich nations have built their wealth and power base by economically or politically abusing poorer people. Where there is terrorism there is always a feeling of powerlessness and injustice. When you as an individual or, even better, two or more people gather together and focus this healing rainbow prayer and visualization between two countries or organizations, the unicorns will gladly support this offering of service.

Disharmony also arises between businesses, religions or even cultures. The unicorns will work with you to help heal schisms. So how do you visualize countries, religions or other organizations? You can either imagine a map with the countries or places marked on it. Alternatively you can picture the leaders. Or you can envision a symbol such as the Bible or Koran or a cross, six-pointed star, swastika, flag, business logo or something that you associate with those involved.

You can even draw it before you start the healing to give more emphasis to your visualization. Recognize that you are part of the oneness and that in sending healing to another, you are healing part of your own soul. We cannot separate what is happening in other parts of the world from self.

EXERCISE: Prayer for Healing of Conflict between Others

I recognize that we are all one and am willing to surrender my conflicts, both inner and outer, my desire for control, my ego attachments and judgements, so that my shift in consciousness may become our change.

I call on the unicorns to open my heart and mind towards you to bring about harmony between you. So be it. It is done.

EXERCISE: Healing Rainbow Visualization between Countries, Businesses or Organizations

1. Sit quietly where you will be undisturbed.
2. Breathe comfortably in and out of your heart centre until you feel relaxed.
3. Ask your unicorn to touch your heart with his horn. Trust that this has happened or visualize this happening.
4. Sense the petals of your heart opening wide.
5. Picture a symbol or person from each of the countries, businesses, organizations or cultures.
6. Imagine your unicorn taking a rainbow from your heart to each of them and then back to you, so that your heart energy links them.
7. Send love and any other qualities you feel inspired to bestow along the rainbow.
8. When you feel ready you can send a message of love, peace or encouragement from your heart. You do not need to know them.
9. After a little while sense how your heart feels.

10. You may have received impressions or even a message from the place or people.
11. Thank all those involved for being receptive—and your unicorn. Then put a rainbow cloak over your aura and open your eyes.

CHAPTER 16

DREAMING OF UNICORNS

❃

When you dream about unicorns, you are meeting them on the inner planes. This means that they are already working with you.

I was chatting to someone I met at a party who told me that she knew nothing about unicorns and had never thought about them. One day she was at a healing workshop where the group was taken into a meditation and she fell into a very deep state of trance. A unicorn appeared to her, so vivid and real that she can still remember the feelings. It did not give her a message; just looked lovingly at her and she came out of the meditation feeling very peaceful yet excited. She wanted to know what the dream meant. As she had been talking about becoming a healer—and unicorns are great healers who work at a soul level, which powerfully affects the physical—I suggested it could be encouraging her to develop her healing skills. I was sure they were calling on her to work with unicorn energy. She felt this was just right.

Marjo-Kaisu loves the unicorns. She dreamt that she was walking along a corridor when a unicorn approached her. She recognized it as one who had previously visited her and was certain that her unicorn friend would greet her physically by standing on its back legs to hug her, so she was waiting for this to happen. Instead a barrier was suddenly placed between them. When she woke she realized that the unicorn had come to give her the message that she was holding back on a particular issue and must now let go and move forward.

It is a mark of her spiritual progress that she recognized the message and was able to take action.

A Black-and-White Unicorn

Here is a unicorn dream which Eeva experienced just as she was falling asleep, in the moments when the veils between the worlds are thin. She saw the black-and-white head of a unicorn. The vision lasted for some time and in her amazement she tried to examine it closely to distinguish all the details. It felt so good to her that she had a great feeling of joy.

I was interested that a unicorn should present itself to her as black-and-white. Usually black and white together is a signal not to take things to extremes or be too 'black-and-white' in your views. It may be a reminder that there are two sides to a question.

However, black also signifies the deeply mysterious. The black Madonna denotes the depth of female esoteric wisdom. It is the ultimate yin colour. So I wonder if the black-and-white unicorn was telling her that she must use her pure light and at the same time recognize the depth of her feminine wisdom.

Another lady called Elena shared that she had woken one morning with a dream of a unicorn running on lush velvety green grass! There was clean, clear water nearby and the unicorn seemed to have gold glitter outlining its head and mane. In the dream she hurried to tell her sister, so that she could see it too. She wanted to share the amazing experience.

Dreams, daydreams or meditations are trance states when it is possible to slip into other dimensions to access different worlds. Marion had been so busy that when she took a few moments off she started to daydream. She saw herself as a princess walking along a path towards a wonderful castle that was sparkling like something out of a Disney cartoon. As she neared the castle two unicorns came to greet her. When she 'woke' she thought to herself, "Now Marion, you really are getting carried away, unicorns? Really!"

Later she realized that in her scepticism she had denied the unicorns, for that night she had a very clear dream that she came to my house and I put my dark blue shawl round her to keep her safe while I challenged a dark force that was threatening. She woke as I lifted the protective cloak from her.

That evening she attracted someone so angry that it pierced her aura, which upset her so much it took two weeks to recover. Then she read one of my newsletters in which I talked of unicorns. At once she realized that she had called them in, then denied them and lost her protection. She sat down immediately to call on them again to heal the pain she had caused herself.

It is also wonderful that she has so many insights and is able to handle her life as a Master.

People sometimes see unicorns in meditation. Anna told me that she was taking part in a one-day silent meditation retreat. At first she could not silence the chatter of her mind and the harder she tried the worse it got. At last she asked for help. And then a beautiful white unicorn came into view. She climbed on his back, held tightly to his neck and he took her to a waterfall, laid her down on a grassy bank and sat beside her, like a companion. She said thank you and was immediately in a calm, peaceful, even blissful state of mind.

At the end of the meditation session she thought, "If only I could manifest a unicorn somehow today." During the lunch break she went into the far corner of the lovely grounds and chose a sunny spot. As she ate her lunch she glanced to the right and saw something white in the shrubbery. She got up and pushed back the foliage — and there was a gorgeous white stone unicorn! She nearly cried with joy.

Light from the Third Eye

We are spiritual beings in a physical body, so we all have a physical life during the day and a spirit life while we are asleep. While we are asleep we visit friends who live far away or are no longer in their physical bodies or are on another galaxy. If we are spiritually ready we attend teaching or healing sessions with the angels and Masters. Many people do not even realize that they are doing spiritual work during their dream times, helping, guiding and rescuing others.

Marjo-Kaisu had this dream recall about one such experience. In her dream she had been taken on a trip to meet some of her cosmic friends from other star systems. They did not have human-looking bodies but they were all very friendly and talked and laughed a great deal. A male creator energy was standing apart from the group. He was very gentle with shining eyes and was simply watching. She knew that he was using mind power and was intrigued that he appeared to have a unicorn horn coming out of his third eye. His message was transmitted very clearly to her. He wanted to remind her that humans must balance the mind and heart. If we are only heart centred we become ungrounded. If we are only head centred we can become selfish and lack compassion. Marjo-Kaisu emphasized again that his energy was gentle and kindly but she was puzzled by the unicorn horn.

I was able to remind her that beams of light from the third eye are emanations of high-frequency thought power. These can be thoughts of manifestation, healing or enlightenment. All pure energy radiating strongly enough from the middle of the forehead can create a horn of light in the same way as radiant heart energies are psychically seen as wings.

Unicorns Conduct the Spirit

I used to have a chat page on my website and Lydia shared this wonderful story about her grandmother, who could see the spiritual worlds. Two days before he was killed in action during the war, her grandfather came to his wife in his spirit body and told her that everything would be alright as he would be near her all the time guiding and comforting her from the other side. Lydia said that she never heard her grandmother complain even though she was left alone with four children and another on the way. She was happy because she knew the Truth. Her doors were open to those in need and she shared her food. She was wonderful with animals and kept cows just for milk and chickens only for eggs, as they were her friends.

When it was time for the old lady to pass over, Lydia's mother woke during the night as she had a dream about the most beautiful white horses, with shimmering silver stars, running around the house and watching through the windows. She immediately woke the family and they gathered round her grandmother.

Lydia wrote: "Her eyes started to shine like stars, looking much bigger, with the most wonderful shades of brilliant blue. She smiled, as she was free—at last she was free to fly with the unicorns." She added: "I was not there at that very special moment but I saw some photos of my Grandmother taken the day before her transition. I will always remember the happiness, joy and love reflecting from her eyes."

CHAPTER 17

WORKING WITH UNICORN DREAMS

Numbers are important in dreams. So, for example, if there are two unicorns in your dream, it may signify that you are coming into balance or that a partner is coming into your life, for it is a romantic number of sharing and togetherness.

Or perhaps there is a unicorn in your dream where five trees seem to stand out. This suggests that you are about to make changes, or run risks and there will be more energy and resources coming in.

The Significance of Numbers

1 — New beginnings, oneness with life, unity, independence, individuality. It suggests you focus all your attention on one vision. It is a very positive number unless you feel lonely or isolated.

2 — This is the number of balance, bringing your masculine and feminine together. It is a romantic, artistic, sensitive energy bringing partnership to you.

3 — This represents the trinity, which symbolizes strength and togetherness. It brings a certain authority, which can be controlling but is hopefully fun. It can also suggest that you have achieved a certain amount but there is more to do. However, with three, you have the strength, self-expression, and openness to reach your goal.

4 — Four is a very stable and solid number, suggesting a good foundation for whatever you wish to create. It often indicates that self-discipline is needed.

5 — This number suggests it is time for change and possibly even a sudden change of direction, which may involve risk. However, you will have the resources you need.

6 — This is a friendly, sociable number. Or it may indicate that you need to devote yourself to a person or cause.

7 — This is the mystical number, so look at your dream from a spiritual perspective. A re-birth might be about to take place.

8 — You have the world at your feet. Eight is the number of infinity and eternity, which often carries power, wealth and cosmic understandings.

9 — This number suggests you may have done very well through your own selfless efforts. It congratulates you.

10 — This is the number of completion, the end of an era, which may give you a sense of self-satisfaction. All is well.

11 — The Master number that heralds new beginnings.

Clearing Your Energy

Before you ask for a unicorn dream, clear your energies and surrender your fear and negativity. This enables your light to be purer, so that they can connect with you at a higher level. Here are some effective ways you can do this.

EXERCISE: How to Clear Your Energy

1. Take a physical bath or shower. As you do so imagine all your fears are being washed away and flowing down the plughole. Singing, chanting or ohming in the water is great.
2. Affirm that you are a being of love and light. Affirm your peace, wisdom, joy and other good qualities.
3. Play a singing bowl and focus on your divine self.
4. Chant or sing sacred songs.
5. Play a CD of sacred music or chanting. The eternal ohm is wonderful for clearing.
6. Walk by water or in a high-energy place like the beach, woods or mountains.

Protection

It is always sensible to protect your spirit when you go to bed at night, so that it can venture safely into the other planes.

You can ask the unicorns or Archangel Gabriel to place a pure white ball of reflective light around you. Make sure you picture it as well as think it.

Alternatively ask Archangel Michael to place his deep blue cloak of protection around you. When you feel the angels placing it over your shoulders, make sure the hood is pulled up over your head and over your third eye. Then mentally zip it up from the floor to the chin.

A third powerful protection is to invoke three times the Gold Ray of Christ. When you stand in the Christ light you are within the protection of the Christ.

Asking for a Unicorn Dream

From time to time during the day think about the unicorns and where you would like to go in your sleep time.

You can ask the unicorns to take you that night to a place where you can learn and evolve. Or you can ask them to help you experience a past life or visit the retreats of masters and archangels—or the unicorn kingdom. Of course, you can tell them that you would like to get to know them better, especially your own unicorn.

If you have a vision, which will help others beyond yourself, you can ask for general guidance or for clarity about your next step.

Prayer

Beloved Unicorns, I ask you to take me in my dreams to ... (place), so that I can release the past/bring back wisdom/get to know my unicorn/receive guidance and evolve and grow for my highest good and the greater good of all. Amen.

Preparing for Sleep

Place a pen and paper by your bedside so that you can write down your dream if you wake in the night. This affirms to your unconscious mind that you are ready to remember such a dream.

Drink a glass of water before you go to sleep. Water is the medium of dreams. It also tends to ensure you don't sleep so deeply that you cannot remember your dream.

Finally think about the unicorns as you fall asleep.

CHAPTER 18

WHITE ANIMALS

Pure white animals, who are not albinos, carry the Christ consciousness energy of pure unconditional love. According to Native American tradition when a white buffalo calf is born, peace will start to come about on Earth. I remember the rejoicing when the first one was born. Now there have been several.

And white, non-albino births are being reported in many kinds of species, indicating that a wonderful shift in consciousness is occurring. Far from being picked on and killed by their own kind or predators, these sacred white creatures seem to be considered special by the animal kingdom.

I opened the newspaper recently and there was a full page spread of a pure white peacock with its tail in full display. It filled me with indescribable joy, not only because it was overwhelmingly beautiful but I also knew that everyone who saw it was being touched at some level by the Christ consciousness. In addition a multi-coloured peacock metaphysically indicates a tendency to ego and love of glamour. A white one demonstrates and teaches the transcendence of ego.

A few days later I mentioned this over supper with the organizers of a seminar I had been giving. One of them responded that she dreamt a cow was giving birth, and after a very difficult delivery, a pure white calf was born. In the dream she said to her sister that in one of Diana Cooper's books she explains the cow is giving birth to the Christ consciousness. She woke with tears of joy running down her face.

I pointed out that all aspects of a dream represent part of us and that the cow she saw in her dream was herself, so a feminine, loving nurturing part of her had now given birth to the Christ consciousness. She was absolutely delighted and felt a deep sense of the truth of this.

Another lady shared that she was building a new road to her home and one day she saw a tiny little weasel, which was totally white, running up and down it.

Your house symbolizes your consciousness, so building a new way to it is very indicative of new beginnings. Seeing a pure white creature on it intimates that it is blessed.

When I was writing *The Web of Light*, which is set in Africa, I went to see the white lions and was touched by their light. I knew they were still ferocious wild animals at one level but could sense that they carried a core of purity and love. And, of course, where there is a pure white animal, there is a unicorn with it, helping it to hold the Christ consciousness frequency while it is on Earth.

Pure white animals can help you in many ways.

A friend of mine is a therapist and healer. She was working with a fellow healer to help a client who had a very serious problem because of an entity attached to her. The entity gained entry because of sexual abuse by an uncle when she was a child and was deeply embedded in her. It had seriously interfered with her whole life.

My friend did her part but the other healer could not get into the client to remove the rest of it. As she was driving along she saw a pure white deer and instantly she knew this was the time to do the release. Calling on the energy of the deer to help her, she put all her concentration into prising the rest of the entity out of the woman. It worked and she was very grateful to the deer for coming to her.

EXERCISE: Visualization to Call a White Animal

1. Find somewhere where you can be quiet and undisturbed.
2. If possible cleanse the space with a singing bowl or sacred music.
3. Light a candle to raise the frequency.
4. Close your eyes and relax by focussing on your breath.
5. Breathe into your third eye, then out of your heart chakra and continue to do this until you feel centred.
6. Find yourself in a beautiful place out in nature, where the grass is green and there are flowers and trees.
7. You may even be able to sense yourself trailing your fingers in a stream and feel the coolness of the clear, sparkling water on your skin.

8. As you relax and find yourself becoming still, you see a white animal approaching. Its heart is blazing with love and peace.
9. Which white animal has come to you today?
10. As it greets you, feel the Christ consciousness enfold you. Offer it your respects.
11. Be aware of the unicorn that accompanies the white animal. The unicorn is nodding to you, sending you love.
12. Their message is love. Breathe it into your heart.
13. You may be aware of orbs of different colours pouring from the white animal and surrounding you. Let them enter your aura and your heart.
14. As this happens you may receive a message of hope, love and encouragement. Just accept it.
15. Remain in this loving energy as long as you need. Then you will notice the white animal and the unicorn withdraw.
16. When you are ready, open your eyes and return to the room.
17. You will need to drink some pure water as you have received high-frequency energy into your chakras.

CHAPTER 19

UNICORNS AND ANIMALS

Unicorns love all people who work with and honour animals. The farmer who genuinely cares for his cattle, sheep or pigs and looks after them to the best of his ability may find a unicorn nudging him to look at a creature that needs attention.

The person with an open heart and quiet mind, who walks with her dog in a natural and beautiful place may be surprised to know that a unicorn is nearby, quietly watching them.

The caring and attentive vet who is helping his or her sick charges to recover might be astonished to know that an angel or unicorn is assisting him to tend to and heal them.

The unicorns pass information telepathically, transcending the limitations of human words. They communicate in the language of light, which contains spiritual information and knowledge. Both angels and unicorns transfer light full of unseen esoteric information and wisdom to you just as the cells of your body communicate with each other by passing light from one to the next.

They also approach and communicate with all people of good intent, who love and are in charge of animals but perhaps lack understanding. They try to impress on them a better way of working with the creatures in their charge.

Unicorns come from Lakumay, an ascended star belonging to the constellation of Sirius. Dogs, horses, and cows too come from Sirius, as do dolphins, who are the High Priests and Priestesses of the oceans and Keepers of Wisdom. Without being consciously aware of it all animals or people have a link with those whose souls originate from the same planet or star system as they do. Naturally the unicorns have a special bond with horses. You may see one gallop among its friends, their manes flying in the breeze. Those who love horses and care for them well are linked into unicorn energy.

I was sent a picture of a beautiful horse with a unicorn orb right on its crown chakra between its ears. His guardian angel orb was also in the photograph.

Where there is cruelty or carelessness towards one of God's creatures, the unicorns withdraw in sorrow and let the dance of karma continue to play out.

Unicorns Teach Animals at Night

The spirits of animals travel at night, just as those of humans do and people often meet their pets, alive or dead, in the inner planes during dreams. Many humans never get beyond the astral planes, the world of emotions, during their sleep time. This is because their emotional life is more prominent for them than their spiritual quest.

There are many spiritual planes and if you are attuned to unicorn energy you may find that you dream you are in a glade of extraordinary beauty being met by a shimmering white horse.

You may even go to the unicorn schools where you may notice that there are many animals amongst the students! It is so much easier for an animal, unsullied by the trappings of intellect and rational thought to enter the spiritual planes. In the non-physical dimensions the life supports of air or water are not needed, so you may well find dolphins listening attentively to the spiritual teachings offered by the great Master unicorns.

Do the Unicorns Work with the Animals?

Yes when an animal's heart is open and it wants to serve the planet in some way, the unicorns will recognize this and come close to assist. The unicorns have encouraged many dogs that have helped their masters or even strangers in trouble.

Elephants in Phuket

There is a wonderful story about elephants in Phuket, Thailand, who served humans during the Tsunami of 26 th December 2004. I wrote about this in *Angel Answers* but I feel it also belongs here.

On that fateful day a group of elephants demonstrated to the world an example of courage and openheartedness. About twenty minutes before the first tsunami wave hit, some elephants became very agitated and unruly. Four of them, who had just returned from a trip and had not yet been chained up, helped the other five tear free from their chains. Then they all climbed up a hill and started bellowing. Realizing something was wrong, many people followed them so that they were out of danger when the waves hit.

As soon as the water had subsided the elephants charged down and started to pick up children with their trunks. They ran back up the hill with them. Once all the children had been rescued, they started to help the adults. After saving 42 people, the elephants returned to the beach and carried up four bodies. They didn't allow their handlers to mount them until this task had been completed and they then began moving wreckage!

Each of those elephants had a unicorn with him, enlightening them to a higher purpose. The unicorns also helped the people that the elephants rescued, simply by their presence and light. In addition, there were many unicorns amongst the shocked and wounded bringing hope and encouragement to them.

Helping Cats

One of the services that a cat provides is to protect its family and home from entities. There are many lower astral spirits, ghosts, thought forms and others floating around. They are either attracted to dark people or places where they can hide or they seek high-frequency people and places that may be able to help them.

If a cat is struggling to protect its family a unicorn will often come to its assistance. It brings such pure light that the ignorant one may sneak away as it is uncomfortable in the glare. Alternatively the unicorn's light may direct the unfortunate being or thought form to a higher dimension.

The Story of the Whale in the Thames

Humans are polluting the oceans. They are using sonar under the waters which disorientates sea creatures, jamming their navigation systems and causing them misery and often death. Because of this many of them are unable to fulfil their soul purpose and destiny. In

2005, one whale was sent as an emissary to draw the attention of the world to their plight. Its progress up the river Thames in London was watched by people throughout the planet who opened their hearts to it.

Because this whale was sacrificing its life for the higher purpose of all the fish and mammals in the ocean, a unicorn stayed with it. It was the unicorn's light that drew the attention of the world and helped raise consciousness.

Do Unicorns Help Birds and Animals to Evolve?

By working with those animals that have a soul desire to serve, they automatically help the creature to raise their frequency and evolve. Also, when a flock of animals or birds is ready to evolve, sometimes through love and grace, the unicorns will send a wave of their energy, to hold the group in the frequency to which they aspire.

Sheer Fun

My friend Elizabeth sent me a photograph of herself on a horse swimming down a rushing river in New Zealand. As I looked at it I had an overwhelming feeling of unicorn presence and was told that one was with them but it was not there to support them. It had come to play because she and the horse were enjoying innocent, exhilarating fun. And the unicorn energy unconsciously added to their joy of the experience—one of the highlights of the trip, she told me.

EXERCISE: Visualization to Meet the Animals

1. Find a place where you can be undisturbed and quiet.
2. Sit or lie and relax by breathing comfortably.
3. Imagine that you are walking along a safe light woodland path.
4. Suddenly it opens out into a clearing.
5. You can see blue sky above and one soft white cloud is drifting lazily across your vision.
6. The clearing is welcoming, filled with sunlight.
7. In the centre is a big, low, smooth, comfortable stone. Sit on it.
8. In a few moments a beautiful unicorn emerges from the trees and approaches you.

9. It lies down beside you and you are filled with a sense of peace and joy.

10. Now other animals are entering the glade with peace and love in their hearts. You may be surprised at the animals you see. You feel totally safe.

11. They form a semi-circle in front of you. Some of them have wanted to talk to you for a long time but now that the unicorn is with you, they can make the connection. Greet them and listen to what they have to say. Take time to converse telepathically.

12. Thank them for visiting you.

13. The unicorn touches you with its horn and then it too leaves the glade.

14. Hold the warmth and love in your heart as you return down the sunlit path, back to the place where you started.

15. Open your eyes and return to the room.

CHAPTER 20

HORSES

Horses are highly evolved creatures, which reincarnate again and again, just as humans do, to experience and learn. When they have mastered all the lessons offered by Earth they ascend. That is when they become a unicorn or a Pegasus.

Jeanne always said how evolved and wonderful her stallion was. He was strong, brave, headstrong and free and she clearly adored him. She was a psychic and medium, able to see and talk to the spirit world. When her beautiful horse finally passed over, she saw his spirit rise out of his body, turn pure white and ascend with light pouring from his third eye. She knew that he became a unicorn!

A lady wrote on the chat page I used to have on my website that she had a very special young horse. One day she really lost her temper and was shouting and raging. She wrote: "My horse was frightened of the noise and galloped round the field for a time, presumably to dissipate my yucky energy from himself. Then he came over to me and looked at me, his eye to my eye, and I got the shock of my life. This is what it must be like for those who look in a dolphin's eye. It struck me that he was older then me, much older, and had been here before. I felt like he was counselling me and I was totally in awe of him." She added that other people who have met him have sensed something about him they can't put their finger on. She believes he is a young horse on this Earth but somehow old and wise beyond Earth years and that he knows more about things than she does. Presumably like many of these wise and beautiful creatures, this is one of those who have mastered the lessons of this plane.

I mention elsewhere that angel wings are the radiations from their heart centres. In exactly the same way, when humans open their hearts they develop etheric wings, which can only be seen by psychics. Very often as someone's wings start to bud and grow, they feel an itching sensation at the back of their shoulders or heart chakra. I have talked to a great many people who have experienced this. Interestingly in many cases, as soon as they recognize and acknowledge that this feeling is the development of their spiritual wings, they relax. Then the sensations caused by resistance stop.

Similarly unicorn horns are emanations of light from their third eye because they have reached enlightenment. Again people who are opening up their third eye often feel sensations, hot, cold, prickly or tingling, in the centre of their foreheads. Sometimes, if I am fine-tuning this spiritual centre or seeking information from the spiritual realms, my third eye tingles or even throbs. On one occasion someone mentioned that my unicorn was touching my third eye with his horn. I immediately felt quite intense pain, partly because I was not expecting it so was unprepared and also because he was opening something that had been locked.

Every horse is a trainee unicorn just as every human is a trainee Ascended Master. When a horse starts to open his third eye, he may want to scratch it against a post to relieve the itching.

Aleja Fischer, who used to be the principal of the German section of the Diana Cooper School of Angels, loves horses. She told me about a time when her beautiful Arab gelding was very ill. The vet wanted to take him to the animal hospital but she knew it was not what he wanted. The family took turns to keep watch over him for two days and nights.

Aleja sat by him in the stable, repeating, "Please don't leave us. We love you." On the third day, while she was giving him healing again, she saw him straighten up. All of a sudden, he sprouted wings and opened them wide. She gasped in wonder: "Oh my, you are a Pegasus!" He responded telepathically: "Yes." Then he settled down and started to recover. She understood that the illness was his initiation into horse mastery. It enabled him to grow into his power and says that he has changed a great deal since then. She said: "Before he was always fooling and playing around, trying to nip at me. Now we have a total understanding. He respects me and is very dignified."

Of course, not every horse is so evolved. Many have only had a few incarnations in this planet and they do not show the wisdom of those who are older souls. They are subject to a normal spiritual growth and progression.

When horses first chose Earth as their planet of growth and learning, they believed they would be free. They generously offered to help humans to travel. Native Americans ride bareback, without reins and this is how the relationship between horses and humans was envisaged. The spiritual hierarchy was shocked and saddened to see horses saddled and bridled, reined and whipped. Horses, with their great strength, volunteered to assist their human friends to do heavy farming work—but they did not expect to be shackled, overworked or even eaten.

Many of these horses, over successive incarnations, became angry, stubborn and bitter. It held back their evolution and we can help them now with prayer, respect and care. Every time you are kind to a horse, you help the entire horse kingdom.

Those who forgave the humans who abused them and maintained their gentle demeanour kept their spirit and evolved through the crucifying challenges, which humans forced upon them. Unicorns, of course, are those who practised forgiveness.

Prayer

I ask and pray that the hearts of humans be open to all horses. Please help us to honour and care for them. Show us the way to live in harmony, love, peace and mutual respect with horses everywhere. Enable us to acknowledge their worth and their mighty spirits. May there be joy and understanding between the human and horse kingdoms.

EXERCISE: Visualization to Honour Horses

1. Take time and space to relax and be still.
2. Close your eyes and breathe comfortably.
3. Picture yourself out in the countryside in a place where you feel totally safe.
4. A beautiful horse is coming up to you. It is peaceful and harmless.
5. Notice its colouring.

6. Connect telepathically with this animal. Greet it and tell it you wish it well.
7. Stroke its nose and pat it lovingly if this feels appropriate.
8. Rub its third eye.
9. Listen to anything the horse wants to tell you. Visualize any action that needs to be taken.
10. Ask if you may ride on its back. In your inner world you can mount it easily. You can also ride bareback, without bridle by holding its mane. You are totally safe.
11. As you are walking, trotting or even galloping with your horse, feel the two of you bonding. Feel its needs and explain yours. Let your heart open. You are learning to act as one.
12. You are heading for a farm where horses have been cruelly treated.
13. Together you are crossing a river, a flat plain and then climbing a hill.
14. When you arrive, work together, safely, constructively and wisely to set them free and help the owner to open his heart.
15. When you have finished, you and your horse are returning back to where you started. Get off and thank your horse. Open your eyes.
16. Know that your inner work has helped all horses everywhere.

CHAPTER 21

THE POWER OF NATURE

Colours in Nature

Unicorns love white for this contains all colours. Each shade is a divine vibration and unicorns appreciate them all. Take a flower. The fairies work with the energies and geometric patterns of most of the colours. The angels can take the essence and light of a wider spectrum and use it to help people and animals. In the inner planes they can weave the colours to give healing. They can help the souls of those who have passed by breathing the colours from the flowers into them.

Unicorns use the finest, most delicate colours, a higher frequency than many of the angels who work with us on the Earth planes can deal with — to soothe and smooth, heal and inspire. They can even use the subtle energy of the flowers to heal your soul or help you find your true divine path. Remember to ask.

Green

Unicorns love this colour, which is that of nature, balance and harmony. And, of course, unicorns are traditionally seen in gentle forest glades or at the end of a green valley. They can take green and weave it into the plan of your life to bring the qualities of balance and harmony to you.

Yellow

One day I was looking at a brilliant yellow gorse bush, which the unicorns said, contained the essence of sunshine, the vibration of happiness. When you see such a colour think about the unicorns and breathe in joy. They will help draw it into you.

Pale Pink and Blue

Tender shades of pink, blue and mauve float in the ethers round the unicorns for they have refined their balanced masculine and feminine qualities. When you find a flower of these colours, take a little time to enjoy it. As you do this be aware that, provided you are open to it, the great-illumined creatures can use the essence of this plant to serve your soul.

Black

Black is absence of colour. It was considered to be the ultimate in feminine magic and mystery. It is the void or cave where renewal and re-birth takes place. Here new ideas can root and develop. When they are ready to sprout and come out into the light of day, the unicorn will help to empower and nurture them.

Silver

The unicorn is often shown as silver white with silver hooves. This is the colour of the moon, which represents the feminine qualities of love, tenderness, nurturing, wisdom and peace. It also denotes time for reflection, contemplation and looking within. Think of unicorns as you look at the moon and expect changes in your consciousness.

Gold

The spiralling horn of the unicorn is often seen as gold, which is the colour of wisdom. It is also the masculine balance to silver just as the sun represents the hot, fierce male energy and the moon the inward, quiet one.

Diamond White

Some very high-frequency unicorns are arriving to help us now and they are sometimes shimmering diamond white, glittering with stars. These unicorns often have platinum horns of light. If you see one know that you are specially blessed for it is helping you to ascend.

Geometric Shapes

If unicorns are looking down on a garden full of shining yellow daffodils, heralding the onset of spring, they will hear the blooms singing in harmony. Someone sent me a picture of orbs round a drumming circle. There were a number of angelic orbs and some of guides but one that I could not recognize. The group was playing with a high spiritual intent and when I asked my guide, Kumeka what the unusual orb was, I was told that it was an ohm, a sacred sound, which had been created by the group with their high-frequency energy. This is how plants sing!

Unicorns will also see that some beautiful flowers are sending out geometric shapes, perhaps upward-pointing triangles. Nearby a cluster of hyacinths may be releasing glorious perfume, wonderful colours and downward-pointing triangles. In the etheric above the garden the geometric symbols merge, forming six-pointed stars, which indicate the bringing of heaven to earth. Where these stars touch people they promote togetherness, harmony, cooperation and oneness.

The symbols float for a while like bubbles in the air and the unicorns waft them gently to places where they may influence people. So much happens that we are not consciously aware of.

A pink rose may send out a heart shape. Certain flowers send out tall thin cube shapes while others send out horizontal cubes. They will seek each other to form a cross.

Different flowers work together, singing like a choir and forming potent symbols. Gardeners of old knew which plants to place together so that they would not only protect or nourish each other but also create divine energies. It is awesome to think that we are literally sending out such powerful lights that can profoundly affect people.

Imagine the magnificence of bright red, twenty-foot tall, rhodo-dendron trees growing on the snow line in the Himalayas. Against the purity of the snow the vibrant flowers are able to send out notes like a million harps in unison in praise of God. And at the same time they emit geometric shapes, which are invitations to look up and see the portals of heaven.

An oak tree can send out an etheric square or cube, which grounds the energies of all in its vicinity. The oak is also a mighty protector of humans and animals.

Unicorns will help those who are ready to come to a suitable place where they can connect with such energies. Many of those who feel inspired to plant flowers in concrete jungles are responding to unicorns. So are those who create glorious gardens.

Roses

Flowers and trees surround and influence us in more ways than we can imagine. For example, a rose will help to dissolve negative influences, including your own thought forms or others sent to you, which smother or attack you. These beautiful flowers will also help to raise your frequency and open your heart. They symbolize love, which is why lovers send roses. When you invoke the unicorns to work with a rose, it accelerates and assists your purification process as well as the opening of your heart.

According to old English legends the rose and the unicorn together stand for strength, constancy and immortality. Mystic art frequently shows unicorns adorned with beautiful red or white roses.

A rose represents the divine feminine. It is the flower of Mother Mary, the divine mother and the unicorn was her familiar or special soul animal.

E X E R C I S E : Flowers and Unicorns

This is something you can do even when it is inclement weather or you are housebound. There is always a way of helping others and the world.

1. Breathe light into your heart and peace out of it.
2. Focus on a high intent.
3. Look at some beautiful flowers or if you cannot do this, find a picture of some on the internet or in a book.
4. As you gaze at them become aware of the energy from them forming an orb of love. What colour is it? What qualities does it contain?
5. Ask a unicorn to take this ball of love to someone you know who needs it.

E X E R C I S E : Music and Unicorns

1. If you are musical or even if you simply enjoy making rhythms, you can use the energy to serve humanity.
2. Imagine your heart is a flower and picture the petals opening and radiating love.
3. Decide where or to whom you would like to dedicate your music.

4. Call in the unicorns and tell them of your higher purpose.
5. Then alone or with friends, ohm, chant, sing or create joyous rhythms.
6. Imagine the unicorns taking the orbs you create, out into the world to help it.

Your body is a sound box. In more peaceful times, villagers used to sing together to keep the community in harmony. In the Golden Era of Atlantis, if your emotions became discordant so that you became vulnerable to ill health, the Priests and Priestesses in the temples would chant you into health and harmony again.

This understanding is returning now and I hear many reports of people healing their organs and bones by humming and chanting. It is generally understood that angels sing with you and over you. Unicorns, although they do not sing, hold the vibrations high as you sing to allow healing to take place. All you have to do is remember to ask them for their help.

CHAPTER 22

UNICORNS AND GARDENS

If you have a garden with a green lawn, however small, where the energy is pure and beautiful, your unicorn will come to you there.

So how can you make your garden more attractive to the higher beings? They love things that send harmony into the atmosphere. This includes flowers, trees and ponds or fountains and anything handmade with love, such as wooden garden furniture. Natural fabrics send out a higher frequency than synthetic ones.

If possible include a bench or seat where people can sit and just be. When you contemplate here, send out peace and love. Sacred or innocent statues, pebbles and crystals all hold and radiate life force and wisdom, which enhance the light of your garden.

Beautiful music, tinkling bells, wind chimes, the sound of water flowing all render your garden more harmonious. The most enticing sound of all is laughter.

Love is a gentle energy, which curves softly and attractively. It is never regimented or straight. So unicorns prefer a natural flowing garden to a formal, angular one.

And they appreciate if possible a little wild part for the fairies and nature spirits.

Those items that send out a heavy energy, such as concrete, plastic, garish colours, and any goods that are made with resentment, bullying or fear repel them. If you have a concrete patio or tarmac drive, place a pot of flowers on it. Do what you can to make your area softer and more natural.

What about Tarmac Roads and Concrete Jungles?

Bless the roads and buildings you pass. Ohm, even if it is under your breath. It will send out good energy. Or play beautiful music or chants as you travel.

Prayer Flags

I have some prayer flags blessed by the Dalai Lama hanging on a branch in my garden. The unicorns love them because the wind blowing through the flags sends out a ripple of high-frequency light.

Planting with Unicorns

When you plant with the unicorns your garden will be more abundant, beautiful and prolific. While you are gardening call in the unicorns to oversee and bless your work. Bless your seeds before you sow them and ask the unicorns to help them germinate. Bless your flowers, bushes and vegetables before you dig them in and ask the unicorns to help them grow. Develop contentment and joy, so that you are radiating these qualities into your plants and the unicorns will multiply this love.

Growing Vegetables

Unicorns understand the symbiotic relationship humans have with their crops. If you love your plants and grow them naturally and harmoniously ask these mighty beings to bless your vegetables and fruit trees. If you know other people who are growing organically and wholesomely, ask the unicorns to visit and bless them too. They will send a shower of stars from their horns of light onto the plants themselves, or into the earth around them if they have not yet germinated. This will enrich the subtle energy of the produce.

When you pass a farm, bless the farmer's fields with unicorn energy. Their light will enhance the prana in the crops. If the farm uses toxic sprays, the blessing will help to mitigate their effect on nature and the human body.

Blessing Sprouted Seeds

One day I asked the unicorns if they would bless the mung beans and sprouted seeds we grow in the kitchen. I felt rather foolish as I asked this trivial thing of these magnificent beings. To my surprise they agreed, adding, "Diana you have often done menial things for others with love in your heart and we will gladly do the same for you." That is a message of love and hope for all of us.

Making a Unicorn Garden

Of course you can dedicate your whole garden to the unicorns and tune into them for guidance. Then you will have a sense of what to place and where to plant. Your intention will call in the mighty beings of light and you may catch a glimpse of them, especially in the moonlight.

A Unicorn Corner

You can choose to create a unicorn corner in a small part of your garden. You could make it with a pond in the centre, on some decking, round a bench or in some bushes or a flowerbed. Make it harmonious, with flowers, pebbles, statues, a bush or two and some water if possible. As long as you create it with the unicorns in your heart, it will be perfect for them.

A Miniature Garden

As a child I loved to make miniature gardens on a plate, with moss for the lawn, flowers, a mirror for a pond. And I would make little benches from twigs and tiny pebbles would form stepping-stones or a path. As an adult, if I make one with my granddaughter, we add tiny model unicorns, angels, fairies and a little Buddha. We dedicate the garden to them. I can feel that it draws the unicorns to us for it is an innocent, fun, creative offering, just the sort of thing that they love.

A Balcony or Window Box

If you do not have a garden, make your balcony or window box into a welcoming, sacred space and offer it to your unicorn. Plant flowers or herbs. Love it and tend it carefully. The unicorns will see how much of your heart and soul you put into it.

An Indoor Garden

If you have no outdoor space to dedicate to the unicorns, create a little indoor garden for them. It is the intention that is important!

An Inner Garden

You have one thing that no one can ever take away. It is your inner world, which is yours to create and enrich as you desire. When you fill your inner world with sunshine and happiness, your outer life automatically reflects this. Here is a visualization to create a unicorn garden, which can be as large or small as you like. You can choose whatever you put into it, so that your unicorn can always find you here.

E X E R C I S E : Unicorn Garden Visualization

1. Find a place where you can relax and be undisturbed.
2. Imagine you are walking safely down a smooth path, so that with each step you take you are becoming more relaxed.
3. There is a gate in front of you and you open it.
4. It leads into an area that is waiting for you to create it into your unicorn garden.
5. Everything you need is there as well as any help you need.
6. Using the power of your imagination you can create a lawn, waterfall, and flowerbed in bloom or anything you want in an instant. Take your time.
7. When you have finished, find a place to relax.
8. Call in the unicorns and explain that you have built this garden for them.
9. They may have some suggestions for you.
10. Ask them to visit you here whenever you go into it.
11. When you are ready, leave your garden by the gate and return to where you started.

Remember

- You can change your inner garden at any time with a brush stroke of your imagination.
- You may prefer to draw your garden on a piece of paper before you visualize it.
- You can invite anyone into your garden that you want to and nobody has the right to enter without your invitation.
- This garden can become a safe haven for you in your inner world.
- The more you visit it the more it becomes part of your reality.

EXERCISE: Reading a Flower

Choose the colour of your flower carefully. If you pick it, ask permission first and remember to thank it, bless it and put it into water when you have finished the exercise. Look through the flower with a slightly unfocussed stare and sense the subtler colours round it. Ask the flower about its purpose. Remember that every flower has a fairy looking after it. Perhaps you can sense it?

CHAPTER 23

UNICORN BABIES

Unicorns have a natural affinity with children and love their company, as they are so innocently open to the inner worlds. I remembered suddenly what Rosie, a psychic little girl of about seven had told me the summer after the unicorns had first come to me. Her brown eyes were shining with excitement and pure joy as she explained that a baby unicorn had been born in her bedroom. She said that its Mummy would not let her play with it for long because it was too young and soon after it was born its parents had taken it away to rest quietly. Then she shared with me its name. She was absolutely thrilled that it was going to be her very own unicorn and she could play with it more as it got bigger. I must confess I heard this story with some scepticism despite the fact that this child has always seen fairies and angels.

I had reason to remember this when I had an extension built on my house. I was intending to pave an area behind the new kitchen. That night the unicorns said they wanted decking, which would not stifle the earth. They also asked for lots of greenery. They added, to my awe and amazement that, because the area I was creating was a sheltered corner they wanted to use it as a nursery for young and baby unicorns.

Baby unicorns! For a split second I felt overwhelmed and honoured. Then my left-brain scepticism and logic cut in. This was crazy—baby unicorns!!! Ridiculous.

I recalled my conversations with that child and cards I had seen with mother and baby unicorns on them. In order to depict little ones the painters must have 'known' at some level that they existed. Now the unicorns themselves were telling me about their babies and expecting me to write about them!! A number of questions came into my mind and I opened up to ask them.

❦

How Does a Spiritual, Etheric Being Produce a Baby?

Unicorns are androgynous, beyond sexuality and with perfectly balanced masculine and feminine energy, just like angels. They may appear as male or female, depending on our need or expectation and, because we project gender onto them.

In order to produce a baby two unicorns hold the spiritual intention of producing another being in their image. Then they 'mate' by merging their energies with this focus. Everything in the vicinity feels the waves of bliss as they unite in a great ball of pure white light. And when they separate a third small unicorn emerges from the energy mass. This new, delicate spiritual energy is nurtured by the older beings.

Why Do Unicorns Have Babies in This Way?

They said it helps them to understand what Earth beings experience when a baby is born.

Unicorns have to lower their frequencies to come to Earth to serve humanity. However, they take all that they learn back to their spiritual home and return it to the Pool of Knowledge of their Kingdom. They tell us that in the future some of them may have to incarnate in a body of flesh as pure white horses, in order to help people remember their oneness with animals. So these experiences are helping to prepare them. That is why the adult unicorns, mighty beings that they are, look after and nurture their offspring.

My Unicorn Nursery

As a result of the unicorns' request I created a beautifully decked private area at the back of my house with a little waterfall, and lots of greenery, softly lit by lights. It is very peaceful and quiet. The builder was marvellous. I told him what the unicorns wanted and he set about making it perfect for them! After six months of working in an angel portal he had opened up considerably to the spiritual worlds. When the extension was finished he sat on a bench saying: "I never want to leave this place."

Why Are Unicorns So Attracted to Babies and Children?

Because of their purity and innocence. They love laughter, fun and happiness, and of course these qualities are magnetic to any light being, but especially unicorns.

The Story of Baby Zeus

This is a story about a baby unicorn shared by Susan Ann: "During Diana's Atlantis week in 2006, she led us into a unicorn visualization. My usual unicorn, Aurora, instantly came in, but I was surprised to sense a second unicorn—a white fluffy baby trotting proudly beside him, like father and son. Aurora introduced me to his young companion, Zeus. 'What a mighty name for such a little unicorn,' I thought.

Since that time Zeus has been at his mentor's side, learning from him, like an apprentice. Whenever Aurora lowers his horn and directs healing through it towards me, Zeus then takes a turn afterwards, imitating his actions. Sometimes I have had to help, for example, bowing down so he can point his short, immature horn at my third eye, or on one occasion I had to kneel so he could reach my solar plexus.

"The energy I receive is different: in the beginning not as powerful or as penetrating as Aurora. It felt more tingly and generalized, as if I was being tickled, whereas that from Aurora was direct, focused and full of sparkles, like a laser beam deeply healing.

"As the months have passed, Zeus has begun to grow and is no longer a tiny cute fluffy bundle with a short stubby horn. The horn has lengthened and he has grown. His healing is becoming more powerful and focused. He is still very definitely a juvenile, but is maturing at great speed and I'm sure he will grow into the mighty Zeus of his name. I feel honoured to have been able to help him in his development."

Fairies and Baby Unicorns

Fairies have a childlike, playful quality and they love to play with baby unicorns. Unicorns are noble and majestic and fairies teach them about fun and lightness. When you sit quietly out in your garden or in the countryside, you may become aware of the two playing together.

Baby Unicorns on Stage

After I gave a lecture a lady approached me and said she had been clairvoyant all her life but had never seen anything to match what she had seen that morning. Apparently there were baby unicorns playing and gambolling all round me on the stage as I talked.

I had to chuckle as I thought about it and was glad I was focussed on the guides and angels who were assisting me. I could have been incredibly distracted otherwise.

EXERCISE: Calling in a Baby Unicorn

As above, so below. A parent does not leave its offspring with someone it does not trust, so it is important to be in a safe and harmless space when you do this visualization as an adult unicorn may come in with the baby! Light a candle if possible.

1. Sit quietly in a place where you can be undisturbed.
2. Breathe golden white light into your heart centre and out of your third eye until you feel relaxed and surrounded in a cocoon of light.
3. Find yourself in a beautiful sunlit garden, with flowers cascading round a pond and birds singing.
4. Mentally send out an invitation for a baby unicorn to come to you.
5. When it approaches you sit still until it gets to know your energy.
6. Then enjoy yourself playing with it and talking to it for as long as you both want to.
7. Tell the baby unicorn you must now leave and call its parent to take it.
8. Then return to where you started.
9. You may like to record your experience in your unicorn journal.

CHAPTER 24

A UNICORN SHOWER

One day I asked the unicorns to work with me while I was in the shower. As the water poured over me, I felt my chakras opening and a channel of light through me. To my surprise the unicorns started dropping etheric white feathers, pearls and petals onto me.

The white feathers are the manifestation of their angelic energy and they felt absolutely beautiful but not unexpected. The petals were white cherry blossom, which I felt symbolized the beginning of something new, perhaps a new start in my spiritual life or a change in my life. The pearls, however, did surprise me.

I could literally feel the feathers, pearls and petals drop through me to settle in various parts of my body and aura.

Since then I have often taken a unicorn shower and commend you to do the same for it is a glowing experience. On other occasions gifts have literally been showered on me. I have received rose petals for love, lilies for higher spirituality and even diamonds for clarity and enlightenment.

It is also a great experience to take a unicorn shower in the rain if you are properly dressed!

Unicorn Shower Blessing

Of course you do not have to be in a physical shower or rainstorm to create a unicorn shower. Simply close your eyes and imagine that gentle water is falling all over you. Ask the unicorns to pour blessings over you and have a sense of what you are being offered. Open up to let the gifts flow into and round your body.

And remember to thank the unicorns.

Unicorns in the Mist

I was walking in my local woods in something between light rain and heavy mist and I asked the unicorns to join me. I asked if it was possible to have a unicorn shower in very soft rain like this. They responded by surrounding me in a rainbow and told me to breathe in the colours, so naturally I did so. They said that people often feel low when the weather is grey, damp and dismal. If you call in a rainbow, they will surround you in its energy and it will give you hope. Breathing in the rainbow light certainly energized me and made me feel very good.

You can ask for any colour you wish, or just let the unicorns in their wisdom send you the shade that is right for you. Imagine a light drizzle of rose pink light or even glowing golden rain that you can absorb!

Pearls

The unicorns said that etheric pearls are formed rather like physical ones. They take the grit of a challenge your soul has undertaken. Round this they place the knowledge and wisdom you have acquired during your efforts to master it. Then they light up the whole with cosmic wisdom and a spiritual pearl appears. I was enchanted by this concept.

Feathers

Unicorns would usually drop a small, pure white feather into your aura. However, if they wanted to send you a special message, they might send you a coloured one.

This might be blue for communication, deep blue for healing, green to balance something in your life, red to give you energy, pink for love or perhaps even gold to suggest you look at a situation with wisdom. If you do receive a coloured feather, physically or in your inner world, recognize it as a blessing and act on the message.

Petals or Flowers

Flower petals contain the energy and life force of the plant from which they come. So if you receive a rose petal you know you are receiving love from the unicorns. If it is a spring blossom, it suggests something new is awakening in you, while a summer one offers energy. For example, if the unicorns waft a golden buttercup to you, it may be that your wisdom is being developed, while a red geranium petal would bring you vitality and a blue forget-me-not might indicate that they want you to remember them!

A snowdrop or white flower would be a message to purify yourself or that you are pure. If you are in doubt, just ask yourself, 'What does this flower mean to me?'

Entering a Pearl

The unicorns asked me to enter one of the pearls they had showered into me, so that I could see the challenge, learn from it and thank it. This, they indicated, would expand my aura and bring me into a state of bliss. This sounded odd to me but I went into meditation and entered the pearl,

I found a beautiful pink and blue pearl in my pancreas and went in through a little door. Inside it was soft and lovely as if I was in a beautiful, warm lagoon. I swam towards a rocky cavern that I could see ahead of me. As I entered the cavern it was dark and forbidding. I shivered. A voice said, "You did not feel loved or valued when you were younger. You had to learn to love and nourish yourself. That was your challenge." In the centre of the cavern I found a tiny premature baby who I recognized was me, feeling unsafe in a huge, loud, hot world. Although her mother was holding her she felt her mother's own fear and lack of self-worth and that was scary. Suddenly I felt an enormous sense of love, compassion and relief. I embraced the mother and the baby and at that the rocks around me dissolved and I was swimming in happiness and bliss in the lagoon.

When I opened my eyes I thanked the unicorns for I knew they had given me a healing.

EXERCISE: Steps to Enter Your Pearl

You may like to do this immediately after your physical unicorn shower, while you are still in the water or you can do this at another time entirely. Water is a very psychic element and people often find it easier to access other realms in the bath. Remember you are in charge and are totally safe at all times. If you are afraid of your challenge, call in a unicorn to help you.

1. Make yourself comfortable and relaxed.
2. Visualize your pearl. How big is it? What colour is it? Is it shiny or dull?

3. If it is in your body, where is it? If it is floating in front of you, that is fine.
4. Find a door at the side of the pearl and go into it. What is it like here? You are in charge and you can explore.
5. If you meet people or animals, talk to them. Find out what they want to tell you.
6. Move towards the 'grit' or challenge in the centre. What form does it take?
7. Enter it and learn about the challenge. You may have impressions, hear a voice or just know.
8. If you need help, call in your unicorn to help you. Whether you feel it or not, he will be there.
9. When you have learnt what the lesson of the challenge is about and have embraced or understood it, it will dissolve.
10. Return through the pearl to the place where you entered.
11. Open your eyes and thank your unicorn.
12. Notice how you feel and, if you wish to do so, note down what you have experienced and learnt.

CHAPTER 25

UNICORN HUMMING BALLS

A humming ball is an energy created by mind focus, sound and colour, visualized between your hands. If you have ever made an angel humming ball, you will know how powerful and beautiful it is. A unicorn one is very similar, except that you create a pure white ball of light and as you hum, you mentally call in the unicorns. Putting your intention into an energy ball, while focussing sound and colour into it, creates something potentially life changing.

Invoking the unicorns at the same time makes it extraordinary. When you have made it you can send it to any person, place or situation. Here are some unicorn qualities you can place in your ball: love, peace, joy, integrity, faith, hope, dignity, serenity, tranquillity, purity, wonder, awe, bliss, perseverance, patience, anticipation and any other aspirations you can think of.

EXERCISE: Making a Unicorn Humming Ball

1. Decide on the unicorn qualities with which you want to fill the ball.
2. Rub your hands together, then hold them a few inches apart (1" equals 2.5 cm), so that you can feel the energy between them. Imagine there is a pure white ball of light between your palms.
3. Tell the unicorns your intention for the humming ball, for example, that you want to use it to send healing to a friend, peace into a situation, integrity to a business deal, or love to open the heart of someone who is hurt.
4. Invite the unicorns to add their energy to your ball.
5. While focussing on the qualities and intention you are putting into your ball, hum into it, sensing it gently expand.

6. Imagine your shimmering ball of unicorn light glowing in your hands.
7. When you have finished ask the unicorns to take it to the person, place, or situation that you envisaged.

E X E R C I S E : Two or More People Making Unicorn Humming Balls for Each Other

If you are with a friend, it is the most wonderful, caring and nourishing thing to make a unicorn humming ball for each other. You can ask your friend what they would like in their ball. One might ask for the ball to be filled with peace and forgiveness, and then placed in their heart. Another might choose unicorn healing and purification for their liver; while another may seek strength and dignity to help them set up a school for deprived children. The possibilities are entirely up to the person who is receiving the ball.

Ask your friend what unicorn qualities they would like in their ball. They can choose several. Also ask them where they want the light to go, such as resolving a relationship, healing part of their body, improving their confidence or to help with a mission.

1. Rub your hands together, and then hold them a few inches (1" equals 2.5 cm) apart, so that you can feel the energy between them. Imagine this is a pure white ball of light.
2. Tell the unicorns where you intend your ball to go.
3. Ask the unicorns to add their energy to your humming ball as you make it.
4. Focussing on the qualities and intention you are putting into your ball, hum into it, sensing it gently expand.
5. Imagine your shimmering ball of unicorn energy glowing in your hands.
6. When you have finished place the ball of light in your friend's heart. You may place it directly into another part of their body if that is what they have requested.

E X E R C I S E : Making a Group Unicorn Ball for a Situation/Person

A number of people may join together to make a unicorn ball for one individual or to send it to a place or situation. Their combined energy is, of course, so much more powerful than if each works individually.

There are several ways of doing this. Either each makes a humming ball as above, and then they merge them together into one large one before they send it. Or they stand in a circle and hold their hands up to energize the big ball they are creating with their light and intention, then they ask the unicorns to take it to its destination.

If you have a hall full of people all of whom are holding the same vision, each can make an individual ball and then send it to the facilitator. Their task is to collect all the energy and direct the unicorns to take it as agreed. I remember once asking about three hundred people to throw me their unicorn balls, so that I could gather them in my arms and send them up to the unicorns. I was almost overwhelmed by the energy.

EXERCISE: Unicorn Humming Ball Circle 1

This is based on the principle that it is in giving that we receive. The more you openheartedly give away love the more it flows into your life.

1. Sit or stand in a circle and make a unicorn humming ball for yourself.
2. Place love or any other quality in it. When your hands are zinging with energy and unicorn blessings, place the ball in the heart of the person to your left.
3. Receive one from whoever is on your right. Because you have created an outflow of love by giving your unicorn ball away, you can accept more into your life.

EXERCISE: Unicorn Humming Ball Circle 2

1. Stand or sit in a circle with one person in the centre.
2. He or she may want to say what unicorn energies they would like to receive.
3. Those in the ring make unicorn humming balls accordingly and when they have finished they place them into the individual in the centre. It feels wonderful to receive!

EXERCISE: Unicorn Humming Ball Circle 3

1. Each person in the circle makes a humming ball.
2. When they are ready they are passed lovingly and meaningfully to the person on your left. In this way each person is receiving and giving.

3. As the unicorn balls go round the circle they gather energy. Finally they are all placed in the centre.
4. Now everyone can breathe in the unicorn energy full of love and intention, taking what they need.

Stories

One lady had always wished to see unicorns but was not clairvoyant. During a unicorn workshop she asked that the unicorn humming ball being created for her go into her third eye with the intention of enabling her to see a unicorn. That very night she had a vivid dream in which her unicorn came to her. She could see it in all its shining glory and has never forgotten that moment.

One woman who was clairvoyant made a unicorn ball and sent it to her aunt. She was amazed to watch it flying through the ethers to her relative. It entered her body, spread through her like warm honey, then re-formed into a ball and flew back to the sender who was watching. It came into her heart and she felt a wonderful tingling cool sensation as the unicorn frequency vibrated there.

Abundance Balloons

I love to give and receive abundance balloons. And under the laws of the Universe you open yourselves up to abundance too. As you hum into your balloon you are envisioning the recipient as if they have already received the riches, success or wellbeing that you wish for them.

I have often seen angels taking abundance balloons up into the ethers to be energized by the Universe. However, I was amazed to see a unicorn carrying an abundance balloon up into the higher realms for its contents to manifest. The unicorns tell me that they frequently take these balls of prayer directly to the higher kingdoms where they can be precipitated into the material realms.

CHAPTER 26

UNICORN ORBS

S ince the advent of the digital camera, orbs, or circles, have become a phenomena in photographs. They appear where there are children, animals, in beauty spots, churches, at ceremonies or celebrations, at spiritual gatherings, portals and other places around the world.

They can be called in by intent in the same way as you can invoke a unicorn. However, the most important factor in the appearance of orbs in a picture is the frequency of the photographer, for they respond to heart energy. Some photographs contain hundreds of orbs or bubbles of light.

Scientists are now saying that these orbs are not caused by a drop of moisture or speck of dust on the lens of the camera but that there is an energy source within each one. This coincides with the understandings of mystics that orbs have a spiritual source.

The planes interpenetrate one another, so we have always been surrounded by spirits. These include fairies, elementals, angels, spirits of the departed, ghosts, spirit guides, Ascended Masters and, of course, unicorns. When I have seen fairies, for example, they are a ball of coloured dancing light, with the shape of a winged being in the centre. This means I see them surrounded by their aura. This light is what is impressed onto the pictures.

Our loved ones in spirit have always visited us to comfort, support, guide or help us. The spirit of a child who has miscarried will often remain around its mother, growing up with the family. A beloved Granny will pop over from the other side from time to time to check on her family. There are also those who do not pass properly and stay attached to the Earth plane as ghosts. All leave an imprint of their presence in the ethers and these are now being caught on film as orbs.

In addition, when the spirit of a human or animal leaves their physical sheath during sleep or meditation, they become part of the spirit world. Interestingly they travel in their light body or merkabah, which is shaped like a three-dimensional six-pointed star. However, as a person evolves their light body becomes softer, more feminine and rounded—an orb.

One of the reasons for the appearance of so many orbs in photographs now is that the veils between the dimensions are becoming thinner. We have been told that proof of the existence of angels and higher spiritual beings will be given to us! I believe orbs in photographs are the start of this.

Different Kinds of Orbs

Some auras are faint and others very bright. Some are small, others large. It depends on their frequency. The solid balls of light are fairies or angels radiating pure love. I am awed how many Angels of Love I have seen in pictures. I have a photograph in which a very bright orb is dancing close to me. This is an angel of love—but much more difficult to see in the same photograph is a unicorn orb.

Other orbs are energy balls containing healing, light, communication or love. These often have patterns within them that are coded messages from the invisible realms. Very often it is the guardian angel or spirit guide talking to that individual.

Learning from Orbs

It was through studying thousands of orbs and learning which ones were unicorns that I discovered more about the unicorns. They are often found working in harmony with angels. They also travel to rescue people who are in danger from negative energy. I have seen an orb of Archangel Michael and a unicorn, merged together, racing to help someone, a trail of energy flowing behind them as they move so fast. They were not in a photograph taken seconds earlier.

I was overjoyed to see unicorn orbs travelling with fairies to help people and sea creatures in a storm that was lashing the coast and ocean. They also help to settle and clear the energy that is stirred up. And most of all I have been delighted to see beautiful unicorn orbs close to the new enlightened children, who can feel and understand their light.

Faces

When you enlarge an orb you can sometimes see a face in it. These are visiting spirits and are always within the light of a unicorn angel or archangel, who is bringing the person to see his loved ones who are still incarnate.

Invitations

As more people are raising their frequency and opening their minds to expanded possibilities, the angels, archangels, Ascended Masters, unicorns and other high beings of light are inviting us to go to archangel retreats or Learning Temples during our sleep.

We travel in our spirit bodies and attend lessons in the inner planes. You can, of course, ask to visit a particular temple, retreat or the unicorn kingdom. In *A New Light on Ascension* I discuss many of the retreats of the archangels and great Masters who are guiding us at this time.

A Unicorn in the Aura

Some years ago I was in Harrogate giving a lecture at a psychic fair. After my talk I wandered through the hall meeting and greeting people. I nodded hello to a man with an aura camera, who recognized me, and beckoned me over. He was taking a lady's aura picture and told me that he could not get the colour to change from red. I could see the screen and indeed her aura was an unrelenting red. She must have been very stressed. He invited me to sit by her and an awesome thing happened, for her aura picture changed to blue and gold.

It was a pivotal moment for me for I clearly saw in front of my eyes what I had always known — that we really can affect other people. There were more revelations to come.

I said to her: "Do you like angels?" She responded that she did. I said: "Why don't you call in the angels and ask them to touch you?" Immediately the screen flashed brighter but nothing else changed.

So I said: "Do you like unicorns?"

Her reply was instant and enthusiastic: "I love the unicorns." "That's great," I responded, "Why don't you call one in?"

Suddenly a ball of pure white light formed on the side of the screen and moved across it until it nestled in the woman's neck, just under her ear. It was evidently unicorn energy and we all felt profoundly affected.

EXERCISE: Calling in a Unicorn Orb

1. Sit quietly indoors or go out into nature if you can.
2. Breathe into your heart and think of a person or animal that you love.
3. Mentally call in the unicorn orbs and ask them to surround and touch you.
4. Be open to the change of energy and sense what is happening to you.
5. Record your experience in your unicorn journal.

CHAPTER 27

UNICORNS AT CHRISTMAS

I have often seen a double row of unicorns in front of my car, rather like those that pull Santa's sleigh. Sometimes there are eight in four pairs. At other times there are an odd number with one in front. I have always assumed that they were protecting my journey and leading the way — and of course they are. But they always reminded me of Christmas and, because unicorns carry the Christ light, they are connected with that time.

A few years ago, when I was writing *The Web of Light*, the third in my trilogy of spiritual novels, my guide Kumeka told me some facts about Christmas and asked me to research others. That was when I learnt that Jesus, whose name was Jeshua Ben Joseph until he attained the name Jesus and was evolved enough to carry the Christ consciousness, was really born in the late spring.

For centuries there was dispute within the patriarchal church about the date to be adopted as his official birthday. In different areas his birth was celebrated any time between January and May. In the fifth century after his birth, at the Council of Rome the holy fathers decreed that his birthday was the 25th December.

This was a highly pragmatic and sensible choice, for that date which was already celebrated as a religious festival in a number of ancient civilizations including India, China, Egypt and Mexico, was the official birthday of many great beings. A number of these were known as sons of God, born of a virgin and their stories included a great star that led wise men to them bearing gifts.

Some of these are Isis, Osiris, Horus, Adonis, Hercules and many of the great Masters. The births of Mithras, the Persian Saviour, Socrates, Aesculapius, Bacchus, Romulus, Krishna, Buddha and Confucius were heralded in this way. Moreover, this date was chosen by the wise ancients because the 25th December is a time of mystical significance, when the portals of heaven open slightly and an outpouring of divine energy bathes the planet.

This means that between 23rd and 26th December high-frequency energy is available to humanity. It is at its peak between midnight on the 24th December until midnight on the 25th. At this time the Christ consciousness can be accessed more easily. And more unicorns pour into the planet at that time to help us take advantage of this wave of light.

I was writing this as the festive season was approaching and once more saw the double row of unicorns in front of my car. I had a sudden flash of them streaking across the sky at Christmas and originating the story of Father Christmas pulling his sledge. Later I sat down to ask about this, certain that the seers of old must have seen this.

I was told that this was indeed the origin of the myth of Santa's reindeers flying through the sky bringing presents as a reward to children for Christmas—though the unicorns never pulled a sleigh. They were trailed by energy, which was interpreted as a sledge.

At this cosmically important time of year when the veils are thin, groups of unicorns respond to requests from countries and communities, who want to make changes for the common good—and where people are ready to put energy into the changes.

They go in groups because the combined energy of a number of unicorns is needed to help activate these prayers.

White Orbs

I have seen awesome pictures of herds of unicorns drifting across the sky, which are captured as pure white orbs. Distant ones appear as shining white pinpricks of light but as they get nearer they have to step down their energy, as it is so pure it would be too much for us. Then they appear as a soft or even faint white orb. If you look at one such picture you will pick up their extraordinary light. If you focus softly on a photograph of unicorn orbs during the Christmas period, a wave of their energy will flow into you.

It is also a special time for single unicorns to visit individuals or families, who have a vision for the higher good and these may be seen as orbs or pinpricks of light across the sky.

Higher Frequencies at Christmas and New Year

A few years ago I was seriously ill in hospital during this precious Christmas period. On Christmas Eve, procedures went on all night so that I did not get any sleep. In the early hours of the morning I was wide awake, when suddenly I saw the Christ light pour in like a waterfall. It was totally awesome as the energy cascaded down the walls, splashed into the room and I knew it was flooding through the wards and spreading through the hospital. What a blessing I received! And I knew that the unicorns were there bringing in the Christ energy for Christmas.

Although this light comes in more strongly on Christmas Day and Boxing Day, it is always available to us.

EXERCISE: Calling in Christ Light

Here is a simple exercise that you can do at any time of any day.

1. Stand with your feet slightly apart, firmly on the ground.
2. Mentally call your unicorn and know it is near you.
3. Open your arms wide to the heavens.
4. Then say or think, "Beautiful unicorns, flood me with Christ light."
5. Wait as you see, sense, imagine or know that Christ light is cascading over and through you.
6. Thank the unicorns.

Unicorns have always loved the innocence, purity and joy of children. Those who saw the sleigh behind the reindeers carrying the gifts to the little ones were seeing the stream of love and purity flowing behind the unicorns. They were bearing the gift of Christ consciousness and joy with which to touch human hearts. Another powerful time to call on unicorn help is on New Year's Eve. Again if your resolution includes a desire to assist others or set alight a vision from your soul, the unicorns will respond. They particularly support the wishes of children at this time.

You can make the invocation and do the exercise at any time but you will receive an additional wave of cosmic energy at Christmas and the New Year.

For the following exercise you will need a candle, paper, pen and crayons if possible. Make sure the room is clean and energetically cleansed. Do the latter by clapping in the corners or using singing bowls or sacred music to break up any lower vibrations.

EXERCISE: Unicorn Wish for the New Year

1. Light a candle before you start.
2. Fold the paper in half lengthways, so that you have space for two columns. Head one, "Thank you", and the other, "My Wishes."
3. Take time to decorate your piece of paper as beautifully as possible, leaving space for writing in the two columns. You may like to do this in silence, so that you use the opportunity to think about the year just past and focus on the year ahead.
4. The more joyous gratitude you offer for the good in the past year, the more you set the energy for something better ahead.
5. Even after a terrible year, look for the sparks of light and the learnings. Write those down under the heading Thank you.
6. Then imagine the most satisfying and joyful things that you would like to create in the next year. Set the bounds of your imagination free and remember that such images are the building blocks of creation.
7. Dream of things that are for the highest good of everyone and notice the feelings of peace, joy, and warmth within you.
8. Be aware that when you serve the Universe and others from your heart the rewards that flow back to you are immense. Don't just picture it.
9. Also write down what you want to create in the following year.

Feeding Your Unicorn

Of course, spiritual beings cannot eat. However, they can take in the energy of something offered to them with love. Think of something you love to eat. It may be a bit of chocolate, a crisp, some fruit or anything you like. Place it with intent as an offering of love for your unicorn. Next day it may look the same but the unicorn will have taken the life force or prana from it as they accept your energy of loving intention and gratitude.

EXERCISE: Goodbye to the Old and Bring in the New

1. First place your offering of food for your unicorn.
2. Say aloud, "I thank the Universe for all the good in my life during last year." Now is the time to read your list.
3. Say aloud, "I now release last year." Turn round three times anti-clockwise to release the old in a powerfully symbolic way.
4. Say aloud, "I wish to create the following in loving service and for my highest fulfilment." Read from your piece of paper.

EXERCISE: Invocation

1. I invoke the mighty unicorns of light to support this vision and to give me strength, courage, love, dignity, confidence, and self-worth, so that I can pour my heart and soul into the coming year. Pause as you feel their white light round you.
2. So be it. It is done.
3. Open your arms to receive your good.
4. You can place your piece of paper on your altar, in a spiritual book or somewhere that you can see and constantly refer to it.
5. Know that you can create your joy and enhance your light in the time ahead.

CHAPTER 28

UNICORN HEALING

Unicorns are seventh-dimensional beings of love and compassion, so of course they have the power to heal.

.Like all beings in this plane of existence, they are subject to the spiritual laws of Earth. If your soul insists that you experience a physical or mental dis-ease because it is the only way you will learn your spiritual lesson, the unicorns must honour the dictates of your soul and step aside. At this time karma is surfacing to be explored and transmuted, so it is relatively rare for a soul to decline healing.

Blockages in the physical body are caused by unhelpful spiritual, mental and emotional patterns, which crystallize to create dis-ease. When the cause is dissolved, the physical adjusts.

When the past is forgiven, released and replaced with higher understanding, healing automatically takes place.

Your heart problem may originate from an inability to forgive someone in this life or from a deeply suppressed fear of being hurt, which came from another life. Unicorn healing so fills your heart with love and joy that there is no room left for pain.

Arthritis in the shoulders may be the result of a lifetime of feeling responsible for your family's problems and resentment that they are dependent on you. Unicorn healing will dissolve your beliefs around being the responsible one. This in turn may set you free to let your family take responsibility for their own lives. As unicorns direct mental or emotional healing to you it will eventually influence your physical body.

Remember, because the beings of light cannot contravene your free will, you must ask for the healing you need.

I was on tour in the USA, catching a different aeroplane each day and was very concerned about my ears, which were suffering because of the pressure. One morning we were taking off on yet another flight and they were already hurting. I asked the unicorns for help and immediately felt warmth over my left ear, which was the more painful one. Then I felt the unicorns pouring energy into both my ears and a wonderful healing glow.

On another occasion I had been sitting in the dentist's chair for one and a half hours and could feel the man's growing tension. No one explained what was going on but clearly something was wrong. I knew my angel was enfolding me and I called in my unicorn too. I could sense he was focussing energy from his horn of light onto the dentist's hands and on my mouth. Despite the assistance of these two amazing beings of light it was an uncomfortable experience. Afterwards my angel and unicorn said I would have lost the tooth, which broke during my time in the chair, if they had not held everything steady. I am really grateful to them.

One day I was talking to a lady who attended a workshop. We were discussing the healing power of unicorns that we both had the privilege of experiencing. Pearl told me that a few weeks earlier she had been absolutely exhausted and as a result felt quite sick. She sat down for a few moments to talk to her unicorn. Immediately she felt it send a wonderful lilac light into her from his horn. Within minutes she felt much better and reenergized.

A lady who worked as a healer told me she was very aware that unicorns were helping her during the sessions. She often saw them working with her and on one particular occasion their presence was very powerful. She was giving healing to a regular client who was evidently very psychic for she suddenly burst out: "Usually you are surrounded by angels but today you have twelve unicorns with you." The healer was astonished and delighted and could only exclaim excitedly: "Oh! You saw them too!"

Healing Children

Apparently the unicorns can connect with you through my unicorn CD and give healing. Here is an amazing story I heard while on tour in South Africa.

A little girl of four was totally traumatized by witnessing her elderly grandparents being brutally beaten up by thugs who had broken into their house. The two-year-old boy slept through the two-hour assault but the little girl saw it all and kept crying: "Please stop." The police could not understand why the assailants suddenly left without even stealing anything.

The four-year-old child was deeply shocked. A year later she wouldn't sleep in her own bed and had constant nightmares. Her parents took her to the doctor, to psychiatrists, psychologists and healers. Nothing helped. Then the mother bought the unicorn CD. She took it home and that night when she put her daughter to bed, she played it. The child listened to it throughout and then fell into her first deep sleep since the attack. She still insists on it being played every night even though she knows it by heart. Thankfully she is now sleeping throughout the night and in her own bed. She is a happy, safe child again.

Thank you, amazing unicorns.

Unicorns Help you Detox

Margaret Merrison was one of the master teachers of the Diana Cooper School and she has a special connection with unicorns. She runs a healing clinic called the Unicorn Centre! When she calls in the unicorns to give healing she feels several of them working together like a team. She said the team looks at the patient and decides who will work where—one on the physical, another on the mental and yet another on the emotional body.

One lady who had received unicorn healing from Margaret said that she went into the most beautiful space and felt the energy working on her liver, detoxing it. Another felt the unicorns pulling strings of guilt and negativity out of her heart centre. A third told me that she felt a tingling, buzzing energy, like a sparkling current and afterwards felt as if the unicorns had lifted a burden and taken it away from her. She felt clearer and more centred and her breathing was better.

Healing of Addictions

I was speaking in Glasgow at the launch of my book *Angel Answers* when Kathleen came to speak to me. She told me that she had attended one of my workshops a year earlier when I had introduced everyone to their unicorns. She said: "In the meditation to meet the unicorns, mine wrapped me as a baby and pierced my heart with his horn. I felt incredibly safe. And from that moment everything changed. I was rid of all addictions—everything; drink, drugs, cigarettes, the lot. I opened up to my spiritual gifts. I became clairvoyant and could feel other people's feelings."

She was glowing with light and I could feel the unicorn presence around her.

CHAPTER 29

HOW TO DO A
UNICORN HEALING

Your physical body is surrounded by a sheath, which is the etheric equivalent of your body. It usually extends about one inch (2.5 cm) around you and this is the level at which many healers work. It is the easiest level of the aura to feel for the others vibrate at a higher frequency.

The emotional body lies between 3" and 6" (7.5 – 15cm) beyond the body. If the unicorn sends light from its horn to a blockage in the emotional body, the patient being healed may feel like crying or exploding with anger as the old is released. Sometimes they will simply feel held in a calm, peaceful space as their energy is purified. About one foot from the body (30cm) you will find the mental body, which is composed of your thought forms. Unicorns can send out light that cuts through or dissolves the tangled beliefs or thoughts that create problems.

The spiritual body lies beyond the mental aura and is usually found about three feet or one metre from the physical, though it can extend up to a mile away in exceptionally evolved people.

A unicorn can see where someone's connection to God is blocked or where they are chained to an illusion that is holding them back, so it can set them free.

The healing process can also work in reverse. When a unicorn sends light directly into the body to dissolve a physical blockage, the stuck emotions and unhelpful beliefs, which created it, start to heal.

When a unicorn gives someone healing it will stay with them for some time, rather like aftercare when you leave hospital. The luminous being keeps an eye on you!

EXERCISE: Giving Unicorn Healing

As with any healing make sure the room is clean and uncluttered. You may like to cleanse it by playing a singing bowl or clapping in all the corners.

Prepare the space by placing a bowl of water near the patient, for this psychic element helps the unicorn energy to connect with both of you. Also, the water draws off any negative energy, which may surface for release when the unicorn's pure healing light enters. Light a candle if you can and play soft music. Flowers too help to raise the light.

Be sure that you are in a good space and healthy yourself.

1. Invite your patient to sit or lie comfortably.
2. Visualize a ball of pure white light surrounding you both for protection and to raise your frequency.
3. Place your hands together in the Namaste or prayer position. This is a sacred mudra and automatically brings light to you. Offer a prayer aloud or mentally. This is an example, "In the name of the Christ I ask for a blessing and healing for _____ (name). I ask the unicorns to work through me. So be it. It is done."
4. Hold your hands up and ask that unicorn light touch them. You may sense them tingling or sparkling with white light.
5. Imagine grounding roots going down from your feet into the earth. Then picture grounding roots going down from your patient's feet into the earth.
6. Place your hands on your patient's shoulders and tune in.
7. Follow your intuition about where to place your hands, either on the physical body or in their aura. Remember this should always be respectful and feel safe and honouring for the person you are giving healing to.
8. To finish, either place your hands on their feet to ground them or place your hands on their shoulders and visualize them being securely rooted.
9. Mentally thank the unicorns.
10. Stand back and make a cutting movement between your chakras and your patient's, so that any cords are cut between you.
11. When your patient opens their eyes offer them a glass of pure water.

EXERCISE: Stroking Your Own Aura or Etheric Body

When you have holes in your aura, which have been created by illness, fearful thoughts or anger, you allow dark energy or even disease to enter.

Taking a few minutes to stroke your etheric body with unicorn hands helps to keep your aura strong and whole. It is an excellent way to keep you healthy. You can do this exercise for yourself quite simply.

1. Hold your hands up and ask the unicorns to touch them with their light.
2. Sense them sparkling pure white and shimmering.
3. Run them down you about 1" (2.5cm) from your physical body.
4. Note you may feel heat, cold or have tingling sensations. Heat indicates congestion. Cold suggests you have a hole in your aura. Take extra care smoothing such areas.
5. When you have finished ask the unicorns to place their pure white protective light round you or call in the Christ light to protect you.

EXERCISE: Stroking Someone Else's Aura or Etheric Body

For this, ask your client to sit sideways on a chair, so that you can reach their back easily. Alternatively ask them to lie down on their back and work on their front. Then suggest they turn over and you can work on their back.

1. Follow steps 1-5 above.
2. Starting over the crown of their head, pass your hands down their body about 1" (2.5cm) away from the physical.
3. Where you feel cool energy, repeat the stroking until the aura here feels comfortable again.
4. Where you feel congestion, you might like to pull stuck energy out—or simply leave your hands over this spot and ask the unicorns to do what is necessary.
5. When you have finished, seal their aura with Archangel Michael's blue cloak of protection or the Christ light.

EXERCISE: Healing the Emotional Body

Follow the steps above but place your hands about 6" (15cm) above the body, where you will almost certainly feel the tingle of the emotional body.

EXERCISE: Healing the Mental Body

Follow the steps outlined above but place your hands in the mental body about 1ft (30cm) from the physical. This usually feels lighter and finer than the emotional body.

EXERCISE: Healing the Spiritual Body

Again follow the steps outlined above but place your hands in the spiritual body. This time start as far away as you can reach beyond the person you are working with and bring your hands closer until you sense their spiritual aura. Usually the patient can feel the energy here more strongly than the other two levels.

Reminder

Pure intention and an open heart are more important than technique. You can only do good.

When healing with unicorns, the most important thing is to move your ego out of the way and let them do the work.

CHAPTER 30

UNICORNS IN ATLANTIS

A tlantis was a cosmic experiment on Earth that lasted for 260,000 years, the longest civilization there has ever been. The continent rose and fell five times. Again and again the culture became technologically advanced but spiritually bankrupt, so that it was terminated. However, in 20,000 BC Atlantis was reinstated for the fifth and last time. This was when the Golden Age arose, a 1,500-year-period during which time the people created Heaven on Earth.

They lived according to spiritual principles, maintained a fifth-dimensional energy and developed very advanced pure crystal technology, which harmed neither the planet nor the people. It was so amazing that it makes our current technology appear infantile.

Throughout this Golden era the people of Atlantis were very psychic and had extraordinary powers. They were all clairvoyant, clairaudient, telepathic and could teleport, apport, levitate, heal and practise telekinesis. Telekinesis is the ability to dematerialize an object external to yourself and rematerialize it in a different place. In those times this was used by everyone to move things. When you apport you dematerialize yourself, move to another location and rematerialize again. In addition everyone could see and communicate with angels and unicorns.

In those halcyon times unicorns roamed throughout Atlantis spreading their divine essence, purity, dignity and light. Everyone had a designated unicorn just as they had a guardian angel.

Nowadays most people agonize over decisions, not realizing that the still quiet thought in their mind is coming from their angel or unicorn. It is the whisper of inspiration, aspiration, hope, courage and love.

In the Golden Age the guidance of these higher beings was clear and direct. Of course, the people had free will then just as they do now but they all wanted to use it for spiritual growth and alignment to the divine. So they listened to the unicorns. And they heard what they had to say.

Because the unicorns are joy-filled, wise and beautiful, all the guidance they offered was for the highest delight and happiness of their charges. The Atlanteans knew this and were full of gratitude and love.

As unicorns and dolphins both originate from the same place, they have a special relationship, so they often communicate and play together. Because the people of Golden Atlantis loved to swim and frolic with the dolphins they built vast pools for them, so that more individuals had access to them. Naturally the people asked the dolphins for permission before they transported them to the pools.

The great creatures were known as the High Priests and Priestesses of the oceans, the keepers of wisdom. As they played with the people, they telepathically downloaded selected wisdom and information into their minds, which they do even today. Often the unicorns would gallop along the edge of a pool or splash through gentle waves by the ocean while the dolphins raced and frolicked in the deeper water. Their combined light helped to maintain the purity of the Atlanteans.

It was only when the energy of Atlantis devolved and became too dense that the unicorns simply withdrew from Earth. They returned to their home planet of Lakumay—and from there they were assigned to help the beings on other star systems where the energy was evolving and the life forms had aspirations to ascend. The unicorns were sent to these places to raise the frequency and help the inhabitants hold their visions.

Previous Eras of Atlantis

In each of the previous ages of Atlantis, there were extremes of dark and light. One group consisted of the Sons of Belial, those who were materialistic and sought sensual pleasure. They were in conflict with the Children of the Law of One, whose lives were dedicated to spiritual knowledge and who focussed on oneness. During all of these times unicorns sought out and helped those whose light was bright. For example in early Atlantis, the priestesses in the Temple of Mary were very aware of the purity and power of unicorn energy. Mary herself always appeared with her unicorn by her side.

Bringing Back Golden Atlantis

At last the frequency on Earth has risen enough for the energy of Golden Atlantis to return. Because of this the Angels of Atlantis, those who were guardian angels of the people of that time and who carry the wisdom of Atlantis, are returning to seek those who are pure and dedicated enough to work with them. These angels have the same vibration as our archangels now. And over the last few years unicorns have once more approached Earth as people have started to evolve again. Many individuals and groups are now radiating bright enough auras to attract the unicorns.

If this chapter particularly interests you it indicates you were incarnated in Golden Atlantis and may be ready to connect once more with the unicorn you knew in those times. Of course, you may already have made the connection.

A Past Life in Atlantis with a Unicorn

A lady shared this story with me after an Atlantis workshop where we all went into a past life. She told me that in a life there her unicorn came to her when she was a little girl. Even at that early age a monk shunned her from the temple, accusing her of being a witch's daughter and saying that the temple was no place for her. In that lifetime her unicorn saved her and guided her. Later she grew into a beautiful young lady with fiery red-blonde hair and her unicorn fought with her against the hypocrites of the temple until she was killed in the fight.

In another life she was again a young woman, this time with three unicorns, one white, one black and the third lilac.

She added that in this life she has been drawn to unicorns since she was a young girl but never understood why. She would wake in the morning, greet the grass, flowers, trees, plants, sky etc. and people thought she was mad. Her unicorns have guided her through this life too, helping her with decisions and life challenges.

Remembering a Life in Atlantis

Because you will have had an incarnation in Golden Atlantis if you are interested in this chapter, it may be helpful to return to a past life there to remember who you truly are. You may want to recall your gifts, re-experience the peace and tranquillity, find out who you were or what you did, make a deeper connection with the unicorn or angel you had then, meet the priests or priestesses or even the High Priests or Priestesses or do something completely different.

If you wish to hold a crystal, charge it with your intention before you start your journey.

EXERCISE: Visualization to Return with Your Unicorn to Atlantis

1. Find a place where you can be quiet and undisturbed.
2. Prepare your space by lighting a candle or whatever feels right.
3. Make sure you can sit or lie comfortably.
4. Ask Archangel Michael to place his deep blue cloak of protection around you.
5. Visualize golden roots anchoring you into the earth.
6. Close your eyes and imagine you are by a beautiful waterfall on a hot sunny day. Feel the spray.
7. Invoke your unicorn and wait for him to come to you.
8. Greet him and thank him for coming. Tell him you would like him to take you back to one of your lives in Golden Atlantis and the reason you want to go there.
9. Ride on his back into the rainbow above the waterfall and fly back over the rainbow bridge to a golden gateway.
10. Climb down from your unicorn and open the gate.
11. As you step through you find yourself in Atlantis, in a different body, in different clothes. Notice what you have on your feet. Feel your robe and be aware of the colour. What crystal are you wearing? Are you a man or a woman?
12. Look around you at the countryside. Can you see any buildings? Can you see people? Animals? What is it like?
13. Let your unicorn take you to the experience you asked for. Take as long as you need.
14. When you are ready, mentally tell your unicorn what you learnt.

15. Allow him to open a door in your third eye with his horn of light. Thank him.
16. Return to the present time to the place where you started. You are exactly the same as you were at the beginning except that your consciousness has expanded.
17. Open your eyes, stretch and make sure you are grounded.
18. Make a record of your experiences in your unicorn journal.

CHAPTER 31

UNICORNS
AND CRYSTALS

O ne of the factors that made Atlantis so extraordinary and unique was the Atlanteans' understanding of crystals. They recognized that crystals have a consciousness and energy that can be harnessed and used. Many of those who were crystal adepts have re-incarnated to bring back their special knowledge.

You can take a quartz crystal, then cleanse, charge and dedicate it to your work with unicorn energy. You can cleanse your crystal in many ways: by playing a singing bowl over it, by chanting the sacred ohm, washing it in water, putting it in uncooked rice or blowing on it. You can charge it with sound dedicated to spirit or with chanting, by placing it by a waterfall or in some other energetic place or by leaving it out in the moonlight.

EXERCISE: Dedicating a Crystal

The setting of the intention is important. Some people like to hold their crystal to their third eye to do this. Here are some suggestions of dedications you could make.

Say the words, "I dedicate (or intend) this crystal to:

1. Connect me with my unicorn.
2. Use unicorn energy to open my heart.
3. Send unicorn healing to others.
4. Energize my unicorn garden.
5. Purify my twelve chakras with unicorn light."

Of course you can make any dedication or intention you wish as long as it is for the light.

You can place your crystal on your altar or carry it round with you. It will be working for you at an energetic level to bring about your vision.

A Unicorn Crystal Altar

An altar is a sacred place, devoted to spirit, and becomes a power spot if the intention and purity is maintained. Even a small altar, such as part of a shelf or small table, can radiate an enormous, high-frequency energy.

When you place your crystal on a dedicated altar, the power is multiplied enormously.

EXERCISE: Making a Unicorn Crystal Altar

1. Find a place, however small, which will be used uniquely for this purpose. You may like to place a special cloth on it, perhaps a golden or white one or a piece of velvet.
2. The four elements, fire, earth, air and water, represented by a candle, crystal, feather and bowl of water or vase of flowers, add energy.
3. Bless any item that you love, such as a shell or photo or picture of an Ascended Master, and place it on it.

The Power of Unicorn Crystal Clearing

You can use a crystal charged with unicorn energy in many ways to purify or clear a place. I know someone who lived in a cul-de-sac where several marriages were breaking up and some violence had occurred. She charged a crystal with unicorn energy and placed it on a street map of her area, on her road. Not only did the separations stop, but some of the couples got together again.

When you work with unicorns, know that the Christ light will automatically replace any negative energy that has been removed.

EXERCISE: How to Do a Unicorn Crystal Clearing

Take your cleansed and charged crystal. Hold it in your hands or up to your third eye and make this intention: "I invoke the unicorns to work with this crystal to cleanse and purify this person (name) or place (name it)."

Place the crystal on a photo of a person. It is enough to write their name on a piece of paper if you do not have a photograph.

Or you can put it on a map, in the centre of the area you want to be cleared. Or you can find a picture of your home or someone else's. Draw a picture of the house or write the address if you have no photo. Put it on a map of the world on a trouble spot or write the name of the place on a piece of paper.

If a river or sea needs cleansing, write the name of the ocean or river and place your dedicated crystal on it or place it appropriately and with intention on a map.

EXERCISE: Unicorn Crystal Healing

Make sure the room is clean and uncluttered. Cleanse it and place a bowl of water near your client. Light a candle, play soft music and place some flowers in the room. All or any of these things will help the energy.

1. Invite your client to sit or lie comfortably.
2. Visualize a ball of pure white light surrounding you both for protection and to raise your frequency.
3. Place into your cleansed and charged crystal the intention that the unicorns work with it to give healing to your client.
4. Imagine grounding roots going down from your feet into the earth. Then picture grounding roots going down from your client's feet into the earth.
5. Follow your intuition about where to hold the crystal in your client's aura.
6. When you finish make sure they are grounded.
7. Mentally thank the unicorns.
8. Stand back and make a cutting movement between your chakras and your client's, so that any cords are cut between you.
9. On opening their eyes, offer your client a glass of pure water.

EXERCISE: Absent Unicorn Crystal Healing

You do this in exactly the same way as you undertake a unicorn crystal cleansing, except for the intention you place in the crystal. You dedicate it to healing. As above you can place a photo of a person under the crystal or you can write the name. You can write the organ that you wish the healing to focus on. However, never specify the dis-ease for you will energize it. Remember to write your experiences in your unicorn journal.

CHAPTER 32

PLANETARY SERVICE

If you have ever signed up consciously or unconsciously to be a planetary ambassador for Earth, one of those who visits other planes of existence, you have exciting work to do. This chapter may help you. If you feel it is not your path, or you think it is peculiar or crazy just move on.

There are many interpenetrating dimensions and planes of existence as well as thousands of galaxies, some with life forms on them. There are those who are much more evolved, spiritually or technologically, than we are and others that are behind us. Some need a great deal of help. Others are offering assistance to us.

When you ask your unicorn to take you to a place in your meditation or sleep where you can be of service, you may find yourself somewhere that feels very unfamiliar. The beings there may look very different from humans. It is not our task to judge or question—simply to serve.

No unicorn would ever take you somewhere too dense or dangerous for you to handle. Nevertheless, as with all spiritual work, you need to wear a cloak of protection and make a clear statement that you only wish to work with and for the Christ light. It is not enough to state that you only wish to work with and for the light as there are many levels of it, some of which are very dim. Asking for the Christ light will keep you very safe.

Remember that this is not a physical operation. It is higher dimensional and works with the power of thought.

You could, for example, ask to take flowers to a place that needed to be lit up by their frequency. Flowers have a healing and heart opening energy. They also raise the vibrational level wherever they are.

I want to share one of my meditations with you. Read it as a metaphor, a tale, imagination or however you want to. If you understand the workings of the Universe read it as it is. It really does not matter for every image has the power of creation and your thoughts affect the entire Universe. This is why positive imaginings and journeys can transform the world.

My Meditation

I closed my eyes and relaxed. Then I focussed on my breathing allowing love to come in and peace to flow out.

First I donned my cloak of protection in which to travel, and then invoked my unicorn, who appeared at my side. I asked him to take me somewhere that I could be of service and said that I would like to take the energy of flowers with me. When he nodded agreement I picked a huge bunch of bluebells and whitebells. Then at the last minute I added narcissi. They smelled wonderful.

I asked my unicorn if I could ride on him and he gave me permission. Then my guardian angel stepped in and wanted to accompany us. I leapt onto my unicorn. My angel sat behind me, enfolding me and making me feel very comfortable. This was not necessary, of course, as she can move anywhere she needs to without riding on the unicorn! So, for that matter can my spirit or yours when not encased in a physical sheath that is subject to gravity.

We flew through the air, which I found exhilarating. Then I saw below a small planet that was surrounded in a grey mist—but there was a shaft of pink light breaking through the cloud. The unicorn stayed behind while my guardian angel and I floated along the pale pink light towards the new planet. We were met by strange looking people, short with grey skin, sharp features and claw like hands. All their focus was on a child who was lying on the ground, looking very ill. Clearly they all adored this little one and because of this, love and compassion had been awakened in them. Their hearts started to open and pink light was pouring from each heart centre. This was the pink light that we saw, which had penetrated the grey cloud above and reached out into the Universe, calling for help. It was to this that the unicorn had apparently responded.

I gave the sick child the bunch of flowers and the effect was instantaneous and startling. He sat up and laughed. The essence of the flowers had touched his soul, so his death wish was transmuted into life force. The people saw this and laughed too. Their hearts suddenly expanded and the pink light became a wide column of energy. It was bright, clear and inviting. Now the unicorn could enter into the higher frequency and arrived among us.

The people were startled by my angel, who had hidden her light under a cloak but nevertheless shone brightly. And when my unicorn arrived in all his shimmering magnificence and glory, they fell back almost blinded.

The unicorn sprayed stars of light and pearls from his horn, which fell on them like rain. As they gathered them up in wonder, we quietly withdrew.

I resolved to return one day to see how they were. Three months later my unicorn, angel and I went back. This time I took four rose bushes — a gold rose for my angel, a white one for my unicorn and a pink one for the love I wanted to take and a red one for energy and vitality.

Now the grey clouds had rolled back. Mist lingered only in patches.

When we landed the people ran to greet us. In front raced a smiling little boy with bright eyes and pink cheeks. The skin of the people was much less grey and I noticed that their flesh had plumped out and their claws had opened as their heart energy flowed into them. They had become hands.

I gave them the roses and explained telepathically what they were for. They seemed to understand and I showed them how to plant and care for them. Of course the roses could not have the physical nutrients that Earth has to offer but now they had huge amounts of love and attention, which is the best nutrient of all.

I was smiling when the unicorn brought me back. As I thanked him and my angel, it felt like a job well done and I was very happy when I opened my eyes.

This was just one of my journeys and if you wish to be in intergalactic service, you can follow these simple steps and do your own work.

⌒

Remember if you ever feel afraid or threatened, simply open your eyes and do something grounding, such as washing the dishes or make a cup of tea. You may never have any concept of the good you have done.

EXERCISE: Planetary Service Steps

1. You may like to think for a few moments about where you would like to go. Or you may prefer your unicorn take you to a place that needs your energy.
2. Prepare your space. Sit comfortably and close your eyes.
3. Relax.
4. Put on your cloak of protection.
5. Invite your unicorn into your inner space.
6. Tell him where you want to go or ask him to take you where you are needed.
7. If he agrees you may ride on his back.
8. Remember you can invite your guardian angel to join you.
9. Let him take you up through the ethers to the place where there is work for you to do.
10. Do whatever is necessary.
11. You can consult your angel or your unicorn or ask for their help.
12. When you have finished, return to Earth to the place where you started.
13. Thank your unicorn and angel.
14. Open your eyes and make sure you are grounded.

If you want to go back to check how the work is going, repeat the process and ask your unicorn to take you there. If you are interested in planetary service, it helps to light a candle each day and dedicate it to the progress of your planetary work.

CHAPTER 33

HEART OPENING

We are now moving into the age of the divine feminine where, in order to progress spiritually, we need to open our hearts. Your unicorn can help you to do this and then can work with you much more readily when you are flowing with love.

Many of us have learnt that it is safer to rationalize, to intellectualize and live in the head. A book doesn't usually jump up and bite you, so you don't get hurt when dealing with logical left brain things. However, you don't truly live either. You miss out on so much of the magic of love. Opening the heart is one of the keys to abundance, to photographing orbs, to communicating with animals as well as receiving more love and happiness in your life.

There are certain things that you can only do with an open heart and these are unbelievably enriching and rewarding. For example, it is almost impossible to keep your heart closed when you are playing with a kitten or puppy. Splashing in a river on a sunny day with a laughing child is guaranteed to open your heart chakra, as is climbing a mountain to look at a magnificent sunset. Unfortunately when you go back into the day-to-day world, it can so easily close again.

However, there are other ways to clear, cleanse, unlock and open your heart to a very deep level. Here are some of them.

EXERCISE: Heart Opening with Rose Quartz

You will need one other person with whom to do this and a cleansed and charged rose quartz crystal dedicated to healing. You may sense the unicorns round you as you work with your crystal.

1. Hold up your rose quartz and ask the unicorns to bless it. State your intention of opening and healing your partner's heart centre.

2. Wind the crystal anti-clockwise over your partner's chest or heart centre, pulling out grief, fear, hurt and all stuck feelings from this and other lives.

3. Hold up the crystal and invoke the Gold and Silver Violet flame to transmute any negativity you have drawn out.

4. Then wind the rose quartz clockwise over your partner's heart chakra, putting in love, hope, happiness, healing, empathy, compassion and joy.

NOTE: If you do this heart opening exercise on yourself, you will appear to reverse the movements, i.e. wind the crystal clockwise to pull out emotions and in an anti-clockwise direction to put light in.

E X E R C I S E : Rose Heart Opening

This is a beautiful exercise and if you are sensitive, you will feel an incredible sensation in your heart centre as the rose in your heart chakra is opened. Both the giver and receiver benefit from this exercise.

It is easier to do this with a partner but if you do not have anyone to work with, practise on yourself. If you are opening your rose alone you may like to watch yourself in a mirror. Whether you do this alone or with a partner, make sure you call in the unicorns and ask them to help you.

1. Imagine there is a rose starting to open in your partner's heart chakra, in the lower middle of their chest.

2. Have a sense of what colour the rose is.

3. Your task is to stroke the petals open very gently. Sense each petal as you open it with your index finger and if you cannot sense it, imagine the petal opening.

4. The delicate petals in the centre may need to be opened very carefully with your little finger.

5. While you are doing this you may intuit or see that there is a bug hiding under a petal. Pull it out and ask the unicorn to transmute it with light from his horn.

6. You may sense or feel that there is a pearl, a diamond, a dewdrop or something else very special nestling among the petals.

7. Ask a unicorn to pour light from its horn right into the centre of the open rose.

NOTE: You may put your own interpretation on anything you discover in the rose but you could consider these suggestions:

- A pearl often means wisdom gained through challenges.
- A diamond might be a beautiful new relationship, situation or project coming into your life. Or it might suggest new clarity about an idea that will result in something good and lasting.
- A dewdrop could indicate new emotions or feelings arising that will enhance your life.

I was once facilitating this exercise at a workshop when one of the participants yelled, "I've found a bug," and promptly threw it on the floor and stamped on it! This is not entirely appropriate! It's much better to send anything you find up to the light.

EXERCISE: Heart Sensing

You will need three or more people for this first exercise.

Version 1

1. One person leaves the room and the others choose a volunteer.
2. They stroke the volunteer's heart rose open as above.
3. When it is fully open, they call back into the room the person who has left.
4. This person must sense or intuit whose heart centre has been opened. They can feel the energy over the heart centres with their hands.

Version 2

1. The person, who is leaving the room, senses the energy over the heart chakras of those in the room. He passes his hand about one inch (or 2.5 cm) above the chest.
2. Then he leaves the room.
3. Those remaining stroke the heart rose of a volunteer open.
4. Then call the person back into the room.
5. He feels the heart aura of each person to sense who has changed.

Version 3

This is a simplified version of the heart sensing exercise. Instead of opening the rose by stroking the petals, focus on the heart centre of the volunteer and ask the unicorns to pour love into it. Notice if the one who has left the room can tell which one has been touched by the unicorn.

EXERCISE: Group Maah

This is a wonderful heart opener especially when you invoke the unicorns to be with you.

1. If you are alone you can take a deep breath, then raise your arms and chant maah from your heart centre for as long as feels right.
2. If there are two or more of you, hold hands, take a deep breath, raise your arms together and all chant maah from your heart centre for as long as feels right.
3. As you do this sense the unicorns pouring the energy from their horns into your heart chakra.

EXERCISE: Looking into Someone's Soul

You will need to do this exercise with another person.

1. Gently and appropriately rub your partner's heart centre to energize it.
2. Place you hand on their chest and look into their eyes. You are now looking into their soul.
3. Say aloud or send telepathically the message, "I love you," three times. If this feels too difficult you may prefer to say, "I see your beauty," or "I accept you as you are."
4. When you have finished, change round.

In families or groups this can bring new understanding, harmony and cooperation. Sometimes people are bowled over by the wisdom and love they sense in their friend's soul.

EXERCISE: Looking into Your Own Soul

If you are doing this alone you will need a mirror to see the true magnificence of your own soul energy.

1. Rub your own heart centre to energize it.
2. With your hand on your heart centre look into your eyes in the mirror and say aloud or think, "I love you," three times. If this feels too difficult you may prefer to say, "I see your beauty," or "I accept you as you are."
3. Notice how you react. How does your body feel?
4. You may have a sense of your unicorn behind you or glimpse him in the mirror.

All these heart opening and soul expanding exercises develop empathy and allow your connection with your unicorn to become stronger.

CHAPTER 34

PORTALS FOR UNICORNS

There are places where the veils between the worlds are thin and here doorways are created where higher beings can access our planet more easily. Such portals occur naturally in beautiful places or power spots, such as mountaintops or great waterfalls. But humans can also make their gardens or houses into angel or unicorn portals—or both.

When the unicorns fly above the world they see the energies rising from all the houses. Some houses have a mushroom of dark energy hovering over them. Many are surrounded by a grey cloud. Occasionally the unicorns rejoice because a shaft of beautiful, clear, inviting light rises from a building. They know that the people who live there are in harmony and are sending love and peace to the world. This can become a portal if these people invite the angels and unicorns to use it. They must, of course, keep it cleansed with intention, singing bowls, incense, love, laughter, prayer, meditation and spiritual practices.

Sometimes a portal of light is created near a dark place, such as a police station, prison or army camp. Then the unicorns are especially pleased, for two reasons. The lightworker has, at a spiritual level, offered to live there to help bring light into the area. Secondly, it enables the higher energies to flow in and help balance some of the aggression.

Sometimes there are dark colours emanating from a house or even a factory or office building. But often there is one person within who is pure. Their prayers or just their light can send a shaft of pure colour up through all the clouds of negative energy. If it is possible a unicorn will enter through this tube of light to help that person. Usually, the being of light will just hold that person's energy, bringing them hope and strengthening their vision. And sometimes this is enough to touch others too. That one light individual has made themselves into a portal. Frequently their bed or desk or favourite chair becomes the gateway.

Where there is a dark home it is usually caused by ignorance exacerbated by the vibration of TV pouring out 'soap' stories, bad news and violent films. In these cases it really helps when lightworkers send light to the situation. The unicorns will take all appropriate prayers and use them to fan any sparks of hope and keep them alive in such a dark spot. Sometimes a unicorn may do something as small as nudging the member of the family with the brightest energy to buy a bunch of flowers or a spiritual book to light up the place. And the same applies to office buildings or any place where people gather.

However, the unicorns can only bring in the lighter energy if there is a pure person in the building. The angels are more able to lower their frequency to enter such a place. Their love is extraordinary but there are many places even they cannot access.

For example, many prisons are cesspools of energy, where people are without hope or grace. It is so important that you send your prayers there, forming sparks, which may some day create a huge flame.

*The higher spiritual beings remind us again and again
that Earth cannot truly ascend until all humans are
ready to light themselves up.*

There are symbols that can be sent to help people everywhere. Some of these are doves, rainbows, stars, crosses of light, feathers, peace flags, or a daisy. Picture one of these and place it where it is needed. The person in agony, emotional despair, at war, or lost will sense it at some level and be comforted.

No prayer or symbol of goodwill is ever wasted. They are all used by the great beings of light.

Making Your Home into a Portal of Light

Goodwill, spiritual practices, and pure intention can turn your home into a portal of light through which angels and unicorns can enter. This is a wonderful thing to create and hugely rewarding.

Everything that raises your frequency will raise that of your home. So prayers for the world, meditation, invocations, dedication of candles to a higher purpose, singing of hymns or bahjans, yoga practice, watching spiritual films, reading spiritual books and talking about angels, unicorns and masters will light up every room.

Of course, beautiful music can really lift the frequency of a place. Imagine the angels and unicorns that arrive when you play gongs or Gregorian chants!

Put a dome of light over your home at night and call in the angels, archangels and unicorns. You may have a sense of them flocking to guard you and bring you love and light. To live in such a home is a wonderful way of keeping the family happy and safe.

CHAPTER 35

SYMBOLISM

Symbols are an expression of something powerful and meaningful. For example, a ring worn on the second finger of the left hand in certain cultures represents union, commitment, fidelity, love, and many other qualities belonging to marriage. A diamond is the concretization of Archangel Gabriel's energy in physical form and contains his attributes of purity, simplicity, light, eternity, and joy. It is a symbol with an invisible force that has meaning far beyond its form. As such, symbols are keys that unlock doors in our consciousness.

While some are universal, containing cosmic energy, others can be personal so you can create your own and imbue it with force and vitality. It will then become a key for you.

Weddings

White symbolizes purity, one of the great attributes of a unicorn. A white wedding used to indicate the chastity of the bride. Now it is more about purity of the heart. Her white veil also portrays the innocence and light of the divine feminine.

In India where the bride is richly dressed in red, she is traditionally carried to the ceremony on a white horse.

The Lion and the Unicorn

In 1603, when Queen Elizabeth I died without an heir, she was succeeded by James VI of Scotland. At that time, the Scottish coat of arms carried two unicorns while the English one bore a lion. The lion and the unicorn were considered to be enemies, which is interesting as the lion represents the male and the unicorn the female! However, they were both thought of as Kings of Beasts. The lion with his masculine energy ruled through strength, might and valour. The unicorn, the feminine, presided with harmony.

When the new coat of arms was designed, in a tactful and sensible gesture, James placed the lion on the left and the unicorn on the right. This symbolized reconciliation between Scotland and England, a merging of their strengths and, of course, the balancing of the masculine and the feminine energies.

The Rose and the Lily

These are the two highest-frequency flowers on the planet. Originally the rose was a symbol used in the West and the lily in the East but over the last few centuries they are both used worldwide. Because of their light and fragrance they are specially loved by unicorns and are often depicted with them.

The Unicorn and the Rose

The rose is an indication of perfect love, bliss and high aspiration. For this reason, the unicorn is often shown garlanded in roses. Together the unicorn and the rose demonstrate strength, constancy and immortality. The rose is the symbol of Mother Mary, the divine feminine. Her soul originates from Venus. Known as the planet of love, it travels in an elliptical movement, which forms the shape of a rose.

The Unicorn and the Iris

The French liked to depict the unicorn with the iris. The former stood for the noble and good, while the blue purple of the flower represented royal bearing. Together they symbolized nobility and loyalty. To some the three petals represent perfection, light and life; to others faith, courage and wisdom.

In France, the iris became known as the fleur-de-Louis after Louis VII, then fleur-de-luce, meaning flower of light and eventually fleur-de-lys, which means flower of the lily. It is considered to be a very powerful symbol and for centuries was used by the French monarchy.

Joan of Arc carried a white banner depicting God blessing the fleur-de-lys, when she led French troops to victory over the English. The iris represents the Virgin Mary. Its three petals indicate the holy Trinity. Apparently, the ancient philosopher Pliny stated that iris should be gathered only by those in a state of chastity.

The iris was also used in Indian and Egyptian cultures to depict life and resurrection. The ancient Egyptians considered it to be a symbol of power and placed it on the third eye of the Sphinx and on the sceptres of their Kings. In Japan it expresses heroism and the colour blue refers to blue blood or nobility.

Iris was highly revered as the Greek goddess of the rainbow, who would take women's souls to the Elysian Fields. As a sacred flower the iris was used in their medicine, for it was considered to have healing powers. The iris is the centre of the eye and symbolically suggests that each of us carries a piece of God within us.

The Story of Our School Logo

For some time our school, the Diana Cooper School, had been discussing what our logo might be. A group of master teachers met at Findhorn, the great spiritual community in northern Scotland, for the annual reunion to discuss the school's progress. One afternoon eleven of the group walked to the point where the two rivers meet, which is the entry point of Archangel Gabriel. For some time we sat on a huge rock at this place, silently watching the river. A huge orange moth, so big that at first glance I thought it was a bird, hovered over the water. As we watched a large fish jumped out of the water and ate it.

A moth symbolizes the negative, the dark, while a fish represents spirituality and is the symbol of many religions. So, in front of our eyes we were shown spirituality consuming the dark.

We stood up and held hands in a circle and suddenly the most amazing thing happened. White light was pouring into the centre of our circle. Mother Mary entered and blessed everyone. Then her unicorn followed her. It was absolutely enormous, the biggest unicorn I have ever seen, a shimmering pure white. It raised its horn and showered light all over us. Archangel Gabriel entered. He gave us a rose, a beautiful white rose with pink tips to the petals, and said it was to be the logo for our school. He told us that we had now earned the right to use this feminine symbol of universal love.

The very interesting thing is that almost everyone had received the rose from Archangel Gabriel before I described it. There were 11 of us, a powerful spiritual number, which indicates new beginnings at a higher level.

Universal Symbols and Their Meaning

Sun – Masculine energy, life force, vitality, happiness.
Moon – Feminine energy, mystery, psychic force and intuition.
Fish – Religion, spirituality.
Bird – Freedom.
Cat – Feminine energy, intuition, psychic force.
Dog – Masculine energy, friendship, loyalty.
Fence – Blockage, restriction.
Gate – Opening to new possibilities.
Ladder – Access to higher possibilities or higher realms. Ambition.
House – Your consciousness.
Tree – Yourself.
Unicorn – Your light, your higher aspect, Christ consciousness.
Yourself – This is you as you feel now.

Do you have eyes to see? Ears to hear—are you listening? Hair is your strength. What is your mouth like? Is it big and red, suggesting you talk a lot or tight and straight, indicating you are quiet or uptight?

Your nose is your intuition. Shoulders carry your burdens, breasts are nurturing. Are your arms open and welcoming or pushing away.

Bridge – Crossing from one state to another.
Path – The route you are taking in life.
River – The river of life.
Vehicle – How you are travelling through your life.
Treasure chest – Contains your gifts and talents.

Is it open or closed? Locked? Large or small?

The list is endless. One fun and informative exercise you can do is a spontaneous drawing, which contains various symbols. It is much better if you cannot draw well as your unconscious mind can then give you messages. A trained artist's skill can disguise the information being conveyed by the unconscious.

When you have drawn your picture, interpret it. It is even better to do this exercise with some friends and take it in turn to comment on each other's drawings.

Interpreting Symbols

If something you have drawn means nothing to you, imagine you have become the person or object.

Example: Perhaps you have drawn a chair. Imagine you are that chair and your unconscious mind has drawn it in a way that gives you a message about your inner world. As you describe it, start sentences with "I feel." You may want to say, "I feel soft and comfortable. I feel too sat upon. I feel hard and rigid. I feel too big for the space. I feel out of place."

To Do a Spontaneous Drawing

Choose five of the above symbols plus a unicorn and yourself. You may have an impulse to use something different, in which case do so. Think of a subject, such as your career, your relationship or your current situation.

Take a piece of paper and draw a picture including these seven items. Very few people can manage to draw a realistic unicorn! It does not matter.

EXERCISE: Interpreting Your Drawing

1. Fold your piece of paper in half. The left hand side as you look at it represents your past, your feminine energy or women in your life. The right hand side indicates your future, your masculine energy or males in your life. If you have a blank on the right you may be having difficulty seeing what your future holds.
   If you have one on the left perhaps there are things in your past that are influencing your life because you do not want to look at them. If the top part of your page is blank what are your aspirations or spiritual understandings? When the lower part of the page is empty you may not yet understand an underlying cause for the situation.
2. If you draw a sun on the left you may consider your happiness or vitality is in the past. If it is in the middle you are focussed on the now, if it is on the right, in the future.
3. The moon is your intuition. It may be full, or new or waning. A new moon may also indicate new beginnings, a waning one that some phase is ending.

191

4. Where have you put yourself? Are you on your path? Are you inside a house looking out or behind a fence? Are you in the centre of your life? Have you drawn your whole body, in other words your whole self? If you have just drawn your head, it may mean that you don't fully understand your role in a situation or that you don't know yourself as well as you might or that you are thinking the situation through rather than feeling it.

5. A tree. What sense do you have of it? Is it strong, fragile, tired, flexible, contained, reaching up, spreading out, filling the space, tiny and insignificant? Is it in leaf, blossoming or bare? Is it leaning to the right? This can indicate that you are orientated towards the future or that you depend on the father energy or a male in your life.

   Is it leaning to the left? This can indicate that you are thinking about the past or that you depend on the mother energy or a woman in your life.

   Or is your tree upright, which means independent?

   Are there roots? If not how can you strengthen your base in life? This may be by making new friends, having more social life, joining an organization or seeing more of your family.

   Are there any lopped off branches or holes, which represent unhealed traumas?

6. Your unicorn represents your Christ consciousness or your light—your higher aspect. How big is it? Where is it? How near to you is it?

There is much more information about interpreting spontaneous drawings in my book *Transform Your Life* including information about colours and combinations of colours.

EXERCISE: Creating Your Own Symbol

This is a unique expression of you. It may be for this moment or you may want to keep it and continue to use it for yourself.

1. Take a piece of paper and choose up to four colours.
2. Sit quietly for a few moments and ask your unicorn to overlight you.

3. Then draw your symbol.
4. If you are working in a group or with someone else, you may like to share what you have depicted and receive their interpretations and projections.

CHAPTER 36

HISTORICAL UNICORN SIGHTINGS

Throughout history, various famous people have reported seeing unicorns in their lives. Here are a few examples of well-known historic personalities.

Emperor Huang Di

In ancient China, a unicorn is said to have appeared to the emperor Huang Di as a sign that his reign would be long and peaceful, which apparently it was.

Emperor Fu Hsi

Apparently the earliest recorded appearance of the Ch'I lin or Chinese unicorn was to the wise and famous Chinese emperor called Fu Hsi, in circa 2900 BC.

By then an old man, he was sitting on the banks of the Yellow River thinking about life and death. He wanted to record his understandings for posterity but writing had not yet been invented. As he sat musing, a unicorn rose out of the water and approached him. It carried on its back magical sigils and from these Fu Hsi devised the first written Chinese language. So the unicorn brought a message from God.

Emperor Wu Ti

A unicorn or Ch'I lin is also said to have appeared to emperor Wu Ti of the Han dynasty, who saw a pure white one in the grounds of his palace.

Genghis Khan

Genghis Khan, one of the most powerful leaders of China, ruled a kingdom that stretched from Korea to Persia. His father was very influential in his life and before every battle, the great warrior tuned into his father's spirit to ask for guidance.

Finally he was ready to invade India with his armies. He and his men had marched for many days through narrow mountain passes and were ready to attack. The story goes that as the sun rose he stood on a vantage point looking down over the country he intended to conquer. A unicorn appeared and knelt in front of him three times in a gesture of submission and reverence while his armies looked on in wonder. Genghis Khan could see the eyes of his long-dead beloved father looking out of the unicorn's eyes.

It was giving him a message not to invade India, the highly spiritual country where Buddha was born. His troops were waiting for the command to march forward but eventually Genghis Khan raised his sword and ordered: "Turn back. My father has warned me not to enter India." He turned his troops round and marched them back across the mountains. India was saved by a unicorn.

Julius Caesar

Julius Caesar wrote in his account of the conquest of Gaul about various creatures that were reputed to inhabit the Hercynian Forest in Germany. One of these he described as "an ox shaped like a stag from the middle of whose forehead, between the ears, stands forth a single horn, taller and straighter than the horns we know."

Alexander the Great

The story goes that when Alexander the Great was a young teenager a Karkadann, a creature with the body of a horse and the head of a lion, was presented to his father. It had a single horn from its brow. All the riders at his father's court tried to ride it and failed. Alexander clamoured to try. Eventually his father gave in, thinking that his son would learn humility.

Alexander realized that this was an animal that could not be tamed but must consent to be ridden. So he approached it without a weapon or whip and stood quietly near him, completely defence-less, repeating: "Greetings, noble beast. I come in friendship. Only permit me to ride on your back today and you may choose your freedom." Slowly the unicorn lowered its head until its horn was almost touching Alexander's heart. They remained like this for some time, then the unicorn suddenly lowered his horn and allowed Alexander to mount. Again they sat quietly getting used to each other. Then Bucephalus galloped away like the wind but when they returned they were inseparable friends, so much so that Alexander rode his unicorn into every major battle.

Confucius

According to legend, a unicorn appeared in 551 BC to Confucius's mother before his birth. This was considered to be a highly auspicious sign. It placed its head in her lap and gave her a piece of imperial jade with the prophecy of the baby's wisdom and future greatness on it. Indeed, Confucius became a venerable and respected Chinese philosopher. It is said that in his old age Confucius saw a unicorn himself.

CHAPTER 37

UNICORNS AND THE BIBLE

The authorized version of the Bible, known as the King James Version, is the only translation of the English Bible that mentions unicorns. They are named seven times. It translates the Hebrew word *re'em* as a unicorn. Literally, *re'em* means ox or wild ox and this is how it is translated in other versions of the Christian Holy Book.

However, on the basis that nothing happens by chance, I tried to translate the concepts metaphysically. This is the only way my understanding of a God of Love could make sense of the words I read, as follows:

- Unicorn translates as Christ consciousness.
- Enemies translate as those of lower consciousness.
- Bones become their very essence.
- Arrows are a force of love.
- Lion's mouth is the point of danger.
- 'Firstling of his bullock' is new and innocent masculine force.
- Blood is life force or joy.
- A calf represents an innocent, generous, lively quality.
- Horns indicate enlightenment.

BIBLE: "God brought them out of Egypt; he hath as it were the strength of an unicorn." *Numbers xxxiii.22*

MY TRANSLATION: God brought them out of Egypt; he hath the strength of Christ consciousness.

BIBLE: "God brought him forth out of Egypt; he hath as it were the strength of a unicorn; he shall eat up the nations his enemies, and shall break their bones, and pierce them through with his arrows." *Numbers xxiv.8*

MY TRANSLATION: God brought them out of Egypt, he hath the strength of Christ consciousness, which shall devour the lower consciousness and transform their essence and pierce them through with the force of his love.

BIBLE: "Save me from the lion's mouth: for thou has heard me from the horns of the unicorns." *Psalm xxii.21*

MY TRANSLATION: Save me from the point of danger for the Christ consciousness has communicated with you.

BIBLE: "His glory is like the firstling of his bullock, and his horns are like the horns of unicorns; with them he shall push the people together to the ends of the earth; and they are the ten thousands of Ephraim, and they are the thousands of Manasseh." *Deuteronomy xxxiii.17*

MY TRANSLATION: His glory is like the new and innocent masculine force, with the enlightenment of Christ consciousness and he shall gather people throughout the world.

BIBLE: "Will the unicorn be willing to serve thee, or abide by thy crib? Canst thou bind the unicorn with his band in the furrow? Or will he harrow the valleys after thee?" *Job xxxix.9*

"Wilt thou trust him because his strength is great? Or wilt thou leave thy labour to him? Wilt thou believe him, that he will bring home thy seed, and gather it into thy barn?" *Job xxxix.9-12*

MY TRANSLATION: Will the Christ consciousness work with you and remain with you? Can you bind and harness the Christ consciousness in the direction you want? Or will it still be there after you have left? Will you trust it because of its great power? Will you let it do the work? Will you believe that it can look after your family?

BIBLE: "He maketh them also to skip like a calf, Lebanon and Siron like a young unicorn." *Psalms xxix.6*

MY TRANSLATION: They will skip with pure innocence and life force, Lebanon and Siron, with Christ consciousness.

BIBLE: "And the unicorns shall come down with them, and the bullocks with their bulls, and their land shall be soaked with blood, and their dust made fat with fatness." *Isaiah xxxiv.7*

MY TRANSLATION: And the Christ consciousness will merge with the masculine energy and the Earth itself will be filled with joy and soul satisfaction.

BIBLE: "But my horn shalt thou exalt like the horn of a unicorn: I shall be anointed with fresh oil." *Psalms xcii.10*

MY TRANSLATION: You will exalt in the enlightenment of Christ consciousness. Everything will appear fresh and new.

CHAPTER 38

EASTERN MYTHS
AND LEGENDS

U nicorns seem to appear in a form that is meaningful locally. In
the East the one-horned magical creature is usually depicted as
a goat, with cloven hooves and a beard. It is gentle and peaceful and
brings good luck.

Interestingly unicorns bring enlightenment and goats originate
from Orion, the planet of enlightenment. A beard has long been a
symbol of maturity and wisdom.

In the spiritually advanced times of Golden Atlantis goats were
revered as enlightened creatures. Because of this they were able
to demonstrate their higher natures. It was only when the church
gained influence that it singled out and distorted the sexual aspects
of reproduction, focussing on the baser emotions of lust rather than
the opportunities for love and transcendence.

Then they demonized the goat, giving Pan, the God of nature, a
goat's head and base disposition. In fact, Pan is a ninth-dimensional
Master, with responsibilities and powers beyond our understanding.
He works with Archangel Purlimiek and is in charge of the whole of
the natural world.

Many of the Eastern stories were recorded by a Greek doctor
called Ctesias who, in 416 BC, went to the court of the King of
Persia and remained there for seventeen years. During this time he
listened to and wrote down the tales told by the many merchants
and travellers who passed through the city where he worked. Ctesias
appeared to think the animals that the travellers saw were physical
beings, and this may have been true of some.

However, others were fourth-dimensional beings, like the Loch
Ness monster and not always visible to human vision.

In India there are two versions of a legend, one of which tells us that unicorns were huge wild asses with white bodies, dark red or royal purple head and deep blue eyes. According to the other version they had the head of a deer (faith and intuition), the body of a horse (higher spirituality), the tail of a lion (courage and strength), the feet of a goat (wisdom and enlightenment), blue eyes (far seeing).

Both versions describe their single horn as being 18 inches long (45 cm), white at the base, black in the centre and with a sharp crimson red tip. The white indicates that it is radiating very pure knowledge and power. Black is the colour of mystery and magic and suggests deep wisdom, while red indicates that the light is sent out with vitality and life force—a mighty beast indeed.

In China the unicorn was a cross between a lion and a dragon, the masculine and feminine combined, representing courage, strength and wisdom. The Chinese unicorn is known as Ki-lin, Ki meaning male and Lin, female. When one is seen it is a very good omen for it comes from heaven bringing peace, wisdom and plenty. Because it is so gentle it walks softly so that it will not crush a blade of grass and it has a voice as pure as a tinkling bell. It is said to live for 1000 years.

It is known as the king of the beasts and a mighty ruler. Sometimes it has the scales of a fish or dragon and at the same time a mane and cloven hooves.

It had a reputation as a dispenser of justice and unicorns were depicted on the back of judges' chairs in the Han dynasty.

This Chinese unicorn only emerged from its life of isolation and solitude to foretell future events, rather like a messenger from heaven. For example, one appeared to tell of the birth of Confucius and his forthcoming greatness.

A unicorn is also said to have come to the mother of Buddha, some accounts say at his conception and others at his birth, to bless him. Under Buddhist influence the Chinese unicorn became gentle, benevolent and pure. It would not even tread an insect under its hooves and could walk on water.

The Japanese unicorn is quite different. Known as Kirin, it has the body of a bull and a wild mane. It is much feared, especially by wrong doers, as an impartial judge. During a trial the Kirin, when summoned would gaze at anyone who was guilty of a crime. Then he would pierce the criminal's heart with his horn. This was meant to be a harsh punishment. However, with higher understanding it is evident that a unicorn, out of compassion, puts its horn of enlightenment deep into the dark heart of a wrong doer to fill it with love, joy and healing.

The Sun and the Moon

There is a story about the lion and the unicorn dating back to ancient Babylon when the sun and moon were considered to be sacred guides. The sun was represented by the lion and the moon by the unicorn.

The lion with its golden hair and round face like the sun ruled through strength. It was considered to be a dominant ruler and it constantly chased the unicorn. The unicorn is silvery white and rules through grace, harmony and cooperation. The lion seldom catches its prey and when it does the sun is obscured, not the moon.

This story affirms that the divine feminine rules supreme.

CHAPTER 39

WESTERN MYTHS AND LEGENDS

D escriptions of mythical creatures are inevitably based on reports from psychics through the ages, about beings that they see in other dimensions. Like angels, elementals and creatures like the Loch Ness monster, unicorns are not physical but they exist in the ethereal realms. From their dimension they can influence and help us.

Western Stories

In the West, our psychics and mystics have always seen unicorns as pure white ascended horses of light. Early Christian mystics understood that they embody the Christ consciousness or pure unconditional love and this became folklore. Unicorns form part of Christian mythology.

The Garden of Eden

The unicorn, according to the Old Testament, is a creature to fear as well as revere. A story I like is that God commanded Adam to give a name to all the animals on Earth. He named the unicorn first, so God gave this creature a special blessing by touching him on the tip of its horn and conferring healing powers on him.

Later when Adam and Eve were banished from the Garden of Eden, the unicorn was allowed to choose whether it would remain in paradise or accompany Adam and Eve into the world of trial and tribulation. Out of pure compassion and love it decided to go with them and was forever blessed. Because it spent time in heaven and on Earth it is associated with purity, chastity, love, and joy.

The Great Flood

There are many legends about unicorns in the Great flood. Apparently they were confident that they could swim through the flood, so refused to enter Noah's ark. They managed to do so for forty days and forty nights by which time they were exhausted. Some birds saw the unicorns' horns above the water and perched on them for safety. Unfortunately, this was too much for the great beasts who sank under their weight.

What an interesting fable. As I understand it, the Great flood referred to in the Bible and other texts was the flood which finally sank Atlantis about 10,000 BC when the civilization became too dark to be allowed to continue. The beautiful unicorns who were present in the Golden Times of Atlantis, could not remain when the energy became too heavy, so they withdrew into the spiritual planes. This story colourfully represents this truth, indicating that the unicorns struggled to remain in service to Atlantis but at last had to let go.

A Jewish folktale tells this story slightly differently, that the unicorns died during the Great flood because they were too big to fit into the ark. This translates as Christ consciousness was too much for the vibration of those on the ark.

Another story claims that Noah chained the unicorn behind the ark and it swam there throughout the forty days. This is the antithesis of the previous tale. Here it is suggested that those on the ark maintained the Christ consciousness throughout the forty days.

Capturing a Unicorn

One thing all the traditions have in common is that the unicorn cannot be captured by force and taken alive. As the unicorn represents Christ consciousness this is hardly surprising, for no one can force love. It has to be gently allowed to enter.

Many stories follow a theme about a hunter endeavouring to catch the unicorn to take it to the King. This is an analogy about the spiritual seeker trying to obtain the Christ consciousness for his higher Self. It cannot be compelled. So according to the fables, a virgin must be left in a forest glade, preferably naked. Then a unicorn will come to her. She can hold him by the horn and be led to the King.

In other words, the Christ consciousness or real love comes to the pure, unpretentious and innocent. Then the Christ can be contained and led to the higher Self. The story also has a second level of interpretation. The virgin represents Mother Mary and this allegory represents her intercession on behalf of humanity to bear the man who was able to bring the Christ consciousness to Earth. She did so with humility, nobility, wisdom, and compassion.

Unicorns in German Myths

I talked at the Angel Congress in Hamburg in 2007 about the Golden era of Atlantis, during the course of which I mentioned unicorns. When I facilitated a meditation about Atlantis, the unicorns insisted on being introduced again to the people they had known so well in those times. The main purpose of the talk was to initiate everyone into the twelve chakras of Atlantis but after the seminar one person after another was thanking me for helping them to meet their *Einhorn* again.

I didn't know then that the German culture is full of stories about unicorns, though I suppose it is hardly surprising in a country which at that time was covered in forests and known for its myths and magic. In the Middle Ages, their palaces and churches were filled with unicorn images.

Virgin Mary and the Unicorn

In the German cult of the adoration of the Virgin, the Virgin Mary was known as Maria Unicornis, Mary of the Unicorn. They must have tuned into the times of Atlantis when she walked everywhere with her unicorn, her familiar or spirit animal.

Story of the Unicorn Cave

This is one variation of a well-known German myth. There is a cave in the heavily forested Harz Mountains in central Germany called the Einhorn-Höhle, the unicorn cave. A wise woman healer lived in the cave and many came to her for healing and advice. Not unnaturally this alarmed and angered the Christian missionaries, who denounced her as a witch. The missionaries had converted a Frankish king to their religion and now they persuaded him to send soldiers, accompanied by a monk, to arrest her.

As the soldiers scrambled up the mountain, the woman came out of the cave and looked down on them with a total lack of fear. This confused the soldiers but, reckoning she was only an old woman, they continued to climb towards her. As they did so, a beautiful unicorn appeared with a wonderful gleaming golden horn. It knelt down in front of the woman, who stepped onto it and they rode away together, leaving the soldiers and the monk confounded.

Renaissance

In the 16th century, by divine decree a wave of higher energy was directed to Earth to try to raise the frequency from the darkness into which it had fallen. This period was named the Renaissance or rebirth and many artists, sculptors and creative souls incarnated to express the Christ consciousness through their art. Much of it still endures and opens people up to the divine. As part of the wave of light directed by Source to the planet, a few unicorns came back for a short while and were seen by psychics or in dreams and visions. These are depicted in tapestries and other works of art at this time. In one mediaeval tapestry the unicorn is seen to be putting his horn into a fountain of water, which symbolizes the Christ healing the sins of the world.

Arthur and the Unicorn

King Arthur is said to have encountered a unicorn. On his first adventure, he ran aground on an unknown shore, where he encounters a dwarf who tells him this story: he and his wife were marooned there many years ago. His wife died after giving birth to a son. The baby would have died, but the dwarf chanced upon a female unicorn with young. She adopted the young infant, allowing him to nurse with her own children. Nourished by this magical drink, the child grew to be a veritable giant. Arthur is said to witness the miracle for himself when the unicorn and her adopted son return. The giant helps Arthur and his company drag their ship from the sands.

The Horn of Plenty

Almost every culture has a myth about the horn of plenty—the original cornucopia and it is linked with unicorns. In one Greek legend Zeus was suckled by a goat. He broke off one of her horns making her into a one-horned creature or unicorn. From the broken horn poured an abundance of good things.

EXERCISE: Tell a Unicorn Story

These are fun exercises to do in a small group. In my experience some people love them and others hate them!

1. Each person in the circle writes or tells a tale or metaphorical story in which there is a unicorn. When you have finished find the lessons and messages for each of you in your stories.
2. One person starts to tell a story in which a unicorn features. After a few sentences the next person takes over and this continues until the story concludes. Then discuss how the message in the story affects you all.

CHAPTER 40

Unicorn Rituals and Ceremonies

Rituals set cosmic forces in motion, for they are based on following a set routine, which is then energized. The words used to light up a ritual are very important, so they must be positive and pure.

Ceremonies call in beings of light and add power to a ritual. Because of this they should always be undertaken with great care and dedicated for the highest good.

To make a ritual or ceremony more potent wear special clothes and choose the colours mindfully. A unicorn ritual can be made very effective by wearing white, though any of the higher spiritual colours, such as gold, violet, purple, or pink, can be chosen equally if they are available.

Having a shower beforehand and washing your hair symbolizes self-purification before the session starts.

Sacred music, prayer, chants, candles, incense, holy water, flowers, even fruit, all increase the light that is being called forward.

An altar as a focal point that lightens everything up and a gold or white cloth is appropriate for a unicorn ceremony.

Dancing and Drumming Can Also Raise Energy

Drink a glass of pure water after the session for during it high-frequency light pours through you, so you will need to wash out old energy and toxins.

Purification

To clear the space you may like to spray angel or unicorn essence or use a singing bowl or gong. Take the spray or sound into every corner if you are inside.

A Unicorn Altar

You may like to build an altar either alone or as a group. Your attitude of reverence and joy as you prepare it is more important than what you put on it. However, a candle to represent fire, a feather for air, a vase of flowers for water and a crystal for Earth ensure that all the elements are called in. It is lovely to place things of importance to you here, such as a photograph of your family and sacred objects such as an angel statue or one of a unicorn. When the altar is ready say a little prayer to dedicate it according to your intention with thanks to the unicorns.

Your intention might be: the sale of your home, a joy-filled New Year, the opening of a healing centre, the success of a business, good-will in the community, the healing of a family or anything as long as it is for the highest good. This might be suitable wording:

- "We dedicate this altar to _____ and call in the unicorns to bless our vision. We thank the unicorns for their love and light."

Candles

Lighting a candle has a magical influence and always raises the frequency. It is wonderful to walk through a path of lit candles, especially on a dark still night, chanting an ohm, with your unicorn walking with you.

Another beautiful ritual is to light and dedicate a main candle to a purpose such as international peace or a happy birthday. Then each person can light their candle from the primary source and return to their position, knowing their light is blessed. Alternatively each person can light their neighbour's candle.

Rose Essence

Unicorns have a special relationship with roses, so this is a particu-larly appropriate essence to choose for a unicorn ritual. Rose essence smells glorious, repels all lower energies and attracts in love.

Take a white or pink candle and rose essence with which to anoint it. Put a few drops of the rose essence on the candle before you light it. Then dedicate it to your vision. Alternatively you can burn rose essence in a burner.

Unicorn Walk as Part of the Ritual or Ceremony

Each person picks a firm leaf. Remember to ask permission from the tree or plant before you do this. With a biro or felt tip pen write a few words to encapsulate the vision you are holding. Then hold your hands in a Namaste position with the leaf between your palms and ask the unicorns to bless it.

You are going to walk, so mentally invoke the unicorns to be with you. Whether you are alone or in a group, move in silence picturing your vision coming true or pray for help to bring it about. Then hum or tone as you focus on your intent.

When you return place your leaf on the altar.

Labyrinth

If you ask for a unicorn blessing, then hold your vision as you walk a labyrinth, this will increase the power coming to you, for a labyrinth is a sacred shape.

A Circle

This is wonderful if there are a number of you. Holding hands as you walk in a circle symbolizes wholeness or oneness. It also means completion. So if this is a ceremony for closure, formation of a circle is excellent.

If everyone sits or stands in a circle, while holding a lighted candle a beautiful energy is formed. It is also special to walk in a circle with each person holding a lighted candle.

If one circle moves clockwise while the other one moves anti-clockwise, you are powerfully winding up the energy.

A Figure of Eight

This is a symbol of eternity. When an individual, couple or group walks in this shape, holding a lighted candle and an intention of permanence and endurance for their vision, that energy will be impressed into their consciousness and the land.

It is suitable for a couple who want their relationship to last, someone who wants their business to endure or a community who are dedicating themselves to long lasting service.

Spirals

Alone or in a group you can wind up energy by walking in a spiral in a clockwise direction. So you would do this if you wanted to increase the energy of your intention. And you can unwind energy by walking in an anti-clockwise spiral, for example if you want to release something from the past.

Walk by Water

If you can walk round or by a lake or pond or even by the sea, the energy of your ritual or ceremony will be enhanced.

Walk up a Hill or Mountain

Walking up hill is very symbolic of climbing the spiritual mountain and accessing higher light.

At Full Moon

Rituals and Ceremonies at full moon are very powerful for you have the force of the divine feminine adding energy. Powerful ancient rituals always took place at this time. Unicorns love when the moon is fullest.

At New Moon

If you want to call in unicorn energy to help you with a new project, such as the conception of a baby or going to university, create a unicorn ceremony at the new moon. The unicorn blessings will help you enormously as long as your vision is pure.

At Waning Moon

If you want help ending a situation or relationship, practice a ritual or ceremony as the moon wanes. Ask the unicorns to help you end whatever it is with grace and dignity.

A Unicorn Blessing

By invoking the unicorns and allowing their blessing to flow from your hands to people, places or situations, you enhance your unicorn ritual.

Who to Call In

You can invoke any of the Masters, angels or archangels to be present at your ceremony and add their light to it. Again where your intention is clear and pure they will be delighted to assist.

Here are a few:

Jesus Christ (known as Sananda in the inner planes), Kumeka, Buddha, Mohammed, Lord Kuthumi (The World Teacher), Dwjhal Kuhl, Mother Mary, Theresa of Avila, Quan Yin, El Morya, Lanto, Paul the Venetian, Serapis Bey, Hilarion, Mary Magdelene, Lady Nada.

Archangels who often attend ceremonies of light are Archangels Michael, Gabriel, Raphael, Uriel, Chamuel, Jophiel, Zadkiel, Metatron, and Sandalphon.

EXERCISE: A Unicorn in a Labyrinth

You can place a small picture of a unicorn or a stone or crystal that represents it in the centre of a labyrinth. Then walk the sacred space if it is marked out on the ground or follow it with your finger on a page.

Pause at the centre to allow the unicorn light to connect deeply into your consciousness. This is very powerful.

The Ritual or Ceremony

1. Decide on the purpose and intention of your ritual or ceremony.
2. Cleanse, prepare and decorate the space whether inside or outside.
3. Create an altar.
4. Shower and wash your hair.
5. Put on clean clothes, special ones if possible.
6. Play music, chant or sing.
7. Light candles.
8. Place a protection, such as Archangel Michael's blue cloak or the Christ light, over each individual and the group.
9. Each person may like to dedicate their candle or place a flower or other offering on the altar, for world peace or some other aspiration.
10. Invoke the unicorns and any other beings of light.
11. Offer prayers, blessings and thanks.

12. Sit or stand in a receptive position to accept the energy.
13. Perform an activity. This could be burning things you want to let go of, writing a wish for something new, winding up the energy for your intention by walking in a sacred shape or even bathing for purification.
14. Gather round the altar and give thanks again.
15. Ground yourselves by imagining roots going into the earth from your feet and sensing the energy running through you into Mother Earth.

These are merely suggestions. There are a million variations and you can all use your inspirational ideas to create a ceremony that includes everyone and lifts the atmosphere.

CHAPTER 41

SPREADING UNICORN MAGIC

When you have made your unicorn essence you can spray it onto yourself to open you up to their light. This enables them to come nearer to you and touch you. It also means that you can absorb their energy at a cellular level, so that their essence can enter your being, where it can affect you profoundly. When you hold the right intention and invoke them to come into your aura, they will do their best to do so. The unicorn essence will assist this and if you want to encourage unicorns to enter your space, you can spray a room with it.

Of course, you can offer it to other people for unicorn healing and connection.

EXERCISE: Making Unicorn Essence

You must create this essence at the full moon and by water. A stream, big pond or lake is preferable but you can make it by the sea if it is tranquil.

You can do this alone. However, more people with the right focus and intent will enhance the energy.

1. Find a coloured bottle, some spring water and a little alcohol.
2. Fill a bowl with the water. If possible this should be a cut glass crystal bowl.
3. Sit round it and think about the qualities of a unicorn.
4. You may like to chant, sing or ohm.
5. Call them in and sense or feel their presence.
6. Ask them to bless the water and visualize one or more pouring the light from their horns into the liquid.
7. Sit in quiet meditation for as long as feels appropriate.

8. Thank the unicorns.
9. Leave the bowl in the moonlight overnight to be charged.
10. Pour it into the bottles and fix it with up to 50% alcohol.

EXERCISE: Blessing Unicorn Pebbles

Some years ago I was given this exercise by the angels for Angel Awareness day. Now I often do it with the unicorns. It is simple, easy to do and very effective. It is a wonderful way to spread the higher energy out into the world.

1. Find a smooth pebble of any size and hold it in your hands.
2. Relax and take your time to feel it and stroke it.
3. Imagine love, peace and other good qualities flowing from your heart into your hands and then into the pebble.
4. Fill the pebble with as many higher qualities as you wish to.
5. Then hold it out to the unicorns to bless.
6. Wherever you place it that pebble will radiate a unicorn blessing, so you may like to put it somewhere that special energy is needed, for example outside a school, hospital, police station or council offices. And, of course, you can pop it outside your home or that of someone you love.

EXERCISE: Painting Unicorn Pebbles

When blessed pebbles are painted or decorated, the unicorn energy is subtly working with them, so this is a lovely thing to do with children. It is a fun, creative way for adults too to enjoy working with subtle unicorn energy.

1. Find several large pebbles and wash them if necessary.
2. Prepare the painting area by covering all vulnerable objects and the table or floor!
3. You may need overalls for children and adults.
4. Light a candle. Play soft music and generally prepare the sacred space.
5. Stand round the pebbles and invoke the unicorns to come in and help you. To do this you may like to hold hands and say, "We now call in the mighty unicorns and ask them to bless these pebbles and fill them with their light." You may prefer

to ask that they are blessed with peace, happiness, patience, or any quality. If you wish to you can each in turn call in a different quality. If you prefer you can all hold your hands out over the pebbles and ask the unicorns to pour a blessing through your hands into the stones.

6. To increase the energy spray your pebble with unicorn or rose essence.
7. Then paint your pebbles and make them as beautiful as you can.
8. Some people like to paint in silence, others chatter and laugh or sing. It is up to you.
9. Remember to thank the unicorns when you have finished.
10. Place the stone somewhere special knowing that its energy will radiate out.

CHAPTER 42

DEVELOPMENT
EXERCISES

These are simple but powerfully effective exercises, which you can practise with others to develop your heart and third eye. They are all designed so that you can use them with children.

EXERCISE: Snail Reading

The purpose of this exercise is to develop empathy. This is particularly good for children. It also helps develop your psychic ability in different ways.

1. Find a snail. If you have to move it, be very gentle and loving.
2. Take a few breaths and relax.
3. Sit still and try to sense the colour of its aura. You can ask yourself what colour its aura would be if you could see it.
4. Imagine what the snail is feeling.
5. If you like you can draw a picture of the snail and choose crayons to colour round it. You may be unconsciously depicting its aura.
6. You can do this with a worm or beetle or any creature.

EXERCISE: Spoon Sensing

You will need at least three people for this exercise.

1. Find a spoon.
2. One person leaves the room.
3. One of the people in the room holds the spoon and fills it with their energy.
4. The one who has left returns to the room.

5. They take the spoon and try to sense who has been holding it before.

EXERCISE: Flower Reading

For this exercise you will need to find a flower, which can be a garden flower or a wild one or a weed. If you wish to pick it, ask the flower for its permission first and sense that it has been granted before you do so. You can do this alone or with others.

1. Feel the aura of the flower by putting your hands an inch (2.5 cm) or so from it.
2. Sense if it is happy, healthy, tired or how its energy is.
3. Become aware of the fairy that looks after it.
4. If you cannot sense this, imagine what colour and size its fairy would be if you could see it.

EXERCISE: Spoon Bending

This is a psychic exercise, not one of force. Many years ago I stayed in a friend's house. He had a son of about ten who had a book of games, one of which was to bend a spoon. He asked me if I would do it with him, so of course I said, "Yes." I was so astonished by the results that I went straight home and tried spoon bending with my evening class. All the ladies bent their spoons in half. The men, who are more left brain, had greater difficulty.

Most only moved a little way. For years I would meet people who had participated in that particular class, who reminded me of it. And many kept their spoons to remind them of the power of their minds. This is so right, for if you know you can do this, you can do anything, including work with the unicorns.

You need a friend to do this with you. Find a spoon or fork that does not bend when you put pressure on it. If it is flimsy you may be accused of cheating.

1. Sit comfortably and relax into a quiet, contemplative frame of mind. Let go of expectation. Simply be.
2. You hold the spoon gently in your non-dominant hand and stroke with one or two fingers of your other hand. Put no pressure on the spoon.

3. Your friend sits by you quietly suggesting the following, which you may need to repeat several times:

"As you stroke the spoon you are feeling more and more relaxed and comfortable and the spoon is becoming warm and pliable. And another thing is happening. With each stroke the atoms within the spoon are moving further apart, so the metal is becoming softer and softer. Yes, with each stroke the metal of the spoon is becoming softer and softer.

Before long you may notice that there is a slight sensation of movement under your fingers as the spoon begins to bend. Your fingers are feeling warmer and maybe the spoon is feeling different as the atoms within the metal change and it becomes more flexible. Yes it is warmer and softer, just beginning to move slightly, ready to bend all by itself. " And so on.

4. After five minutes or so you may have a spoon that has bent double.

EXERCISE: Crystal Hugging or Stroking

Cleanse your crystals. You can do this by playing a singing bowl, wafting them with a joss stick or even chanting an ohm over them.

1. If you have some big crystals, each person can choose one and hug it.
2. If you have smaller crystals each person chooses one and strokes it.
3. Then hold your palm an inch (2.5 cm) away from it and feel whether it is radiating cool or warm energy.
4. Does it feel alive or dead? What colour is round it?
5. Is the elemental of the crystal communicating with you?
6. When each person has spent time with their crystal, share what you experienced.
7. Then thank your crystal.
8. Cleanse them again and swap crystals, so that you can experience what a different one feels like.

EXERCISE: Find the Unicorn

This is a game to encourage and develop sensitivity to energies. You will need at least three people. It is very good for children.

1. One person leaves the room.
2. The others decide who is to invoke angels and who is to invoke unicorns.
3. They stand in the angel corner or the unicorn corner and do their invocations.
4. Then they call back the person who has left the room.
5. He enters and feels the energy in each corner to sense who are angels and who are unicorns.

EXERCISE: Find the Unicorn for Two People

If you only have two people, one sits quietly while the other invokes either angels or unicorns. When he feels he has absorbed the energy, the other comes and feels his energy fields to sense if he has called in angel energy or that of the unicorns.

EXERCISE: Unicorn Song

This is a wonderful exercise to bring a group into harmony and bring in the unicorn energy. It is fun for a large number of people but you can do it with just two.

For a Large Group

1. Divide into four sections, A, B, C and D, each going to a separate room or space.
2. Each group dedicates this session to unicorn connection.
3. Each creates and practices a unicorn tune or tones. This may take ten minutes or more, so make sure you leave plenty of time.
4. When the groups are ready they return to the main room.
5. Group A sings their tune or tones.
6. Group B joins in, harmonizing with A.
7. Groups C and D join in their turn, all harmonizing.
8. Sense or feel the unicorns with you as you enjoy the sounds.

For a Small Group

1. If there are only two people, each makes up a tune or tones, then they combine to harmonize them.

EXERCISE: Unicorn Song and Movement

Divide into four sections as above. This time each group does a simple movement to the tune or tones and they bring it all together.

CHAPTER 43

UNICORN GAMES
FOR CHILDREN

All these suggestions are to bring more awareness of unicorns to children.

EXERCISE: Paint a Unicorn Picture

It is important to talk about or think about unicorns as you do this.

1. Trace a picture of a unicorn, either from this book or the website—or draw one.
2. What colour do you want your unicorn to be? If it is white, leave it blank, if it is a colour, paint or crayon it in.
3. Draw in your own background and colour it.
4. When you have finished ask your mother to put it up somewhere.

Of course adults can draw and colour unicorns too.

EXERCISE: Pairs or Pelmanism

You can do this with an ordinary deck of cards or with sets of cards of pairs. When my children were small we played this as a game to develop memory. I soon realized it did much more than this, for my son from the age of two began to pick up the entire set by sensing which the pairs were. It tuned his psychic ability.

Remember this is not a competition. The more you can relax the easier you will find it.

You can do this with one or more persons. If you practise alone, make a note of how many turns you need to pick up every pair.

1. Before you begin, relax and tune in. The more comfortable you are the more you can hone your memory and psychic ability.
2. Spread the cards out face down. When you first start use only six pairs. Then increase the number as you get better.
3. The first person picks up two cards and turns them face up. If they match, he takes them. If they do not he returns them, face down, to the place from which he picked them up.
4. The second person can also pick up two cards. Again if they match, they are his.
5. The person with the most pairs at the end of the game is the winner.
6. The more you practise this the more you develop your psychic ability.

EXERCISE: Tray Game

To develop clairvoyance and memory. This game is for one or more players. By relaxing beforehand and opening up your right brain to make an overall picture of the objects on the tray you can develop clairvoyance.

In order to make it a unicorn tray game choose objects that are related to them, for example a white pebble, a flower, a feather, a model horse, a shell or pearl, something to symbolize wings, crystals. And you can add an apple or carrot for while unicorns cannot eat or taste, they can smell and they love the fragrance of apples and carrots.

There are three ways of remembering.

1. Quickly make up a story, which includes each object as a way of remembering them. If you do this, you are using your right as well as your left brain.
2. Concentrate and commit the objects to your short-term memory. In this case you are using your left brain.
3. Relax and scan the tray in soft focus, so that a general picture goes into your right brain.

Practise playing this game in different ways.

1. One person collects a tray of objects and brings them into the room with a cloth over them.

2. Before you begin, take a few breaths and relax.
3. The cloth is taken off for 15 to 30 seconds depending on the ages of the participants. Then it is replaced.
4. Write down as many objects you can remember.

Another version of this exercise is to look at the tray of objects. Then one is removed. Which one is it?

EXERCISE: Variation on the Tray Game

Each person takes an object from the tray. They take it in turns to tell a story about it, do a drawing or make up a poem or song. Of course, each one must include a unicorn.

Sensing Blind Man's Buff

1. One person closes their eyes or is blindfolded.
2. The others stand in different parts of the room or in each corner.
3. The blind man carefully approaches each person and feels their energy field but does not touch anyone.
4. He tries to identify everyone by their energy.

Sound and Sensing Blind Man's Buff

To make the above easier, those being found can hum as the blind man approaches. But he must still identify each person without touching them.

EXERCISE: Unicorn Feather Hunt for Children

The aim of this is to give children a reminder about angel and unicorn feathers and to have fun.

Collect little white feathers from your garden or when you go for a walk. You can also buy packs of white feathers. Explain to the children that unicorns as well as angels leave them to say they have been near you. Hide the feathers in your garden or park. When they are hidden let the children find them.

Depending on the age of the children they could receive a sticker for each one they find. Then they can make a picture with their feathers and stickers. Or each child can receive a small gift. Or you can play it for pleasure without extra reward!

EXERCISE: Unicorn Trail

Chief Unicorn (an adult or older child) lays a trail of white feathers or organically dissolving white petals for the others to follow. They just might see a unicorn as they follow the trail.

EXERCISE: Unicorn Biscuits

Give each child a plain biscuit. Let them decorate it with icing. Older children can pipe unicorn stars onto it or even trace the outline of a unicorn in icing or little silver balls.

EXERCISE: Making a Unicorn Garden

1. For your base, either fill a low bowl with moss or use wet oasis. You can use a small mirror or silver foil for a little pond or stream.
2. Small pebbles make a path.
3. Twigs make trees, which can be painted. Small fir cones are a pretty addition.
4. Dried or fresh flowers. Remember to ask them first for permission to pick them.
5. If you have model farmyard animals, a horse can represent a unicorn.
6. Little toy people. Other animals.
7. Anything else small that you can think of.

EXERCISE: Woodland Glade

You can create a woodland glade as above, using leaves and twigs for trees and perhaps cut out some fairies or make plasticine toadstools into a fairy ring.

EXERCISE: Well Done

Every child loves to be appreciated and reminded of the good they have done. And, of course, by far the quickest way of developing positive qualities in children is to focus on them.

At bedtime my daughter has a 'well-done' session with her five-year-old daughter and two-year-old son. She sits on the bed and names good things they have done, adding 'Well done'. My little grandchildren glow and I know it is an important part of their bedtime routine. If I am there I can always think of lots of 'Well dones' to add! Unicorns love the innocence and purity of children, so ask them to add their blessings and their light as you do this.

Here are a few 'Well dones', though there are any number depending on the child and the circumstances.

- Well done for being polite to Mrs. So and So.
- Well done for answering the phone so well.
- Well done for looking after your baby brother.
- Well done for eating your dinner so well.
- Well done for saying thank you so nicely.
- Well done for not making a fuss when we couldn't go out as promised.
- Well done for doing such good colouring in.
- Well done for being kind to the child next door.
- Well done for sharing your toys.
- And 'Well dones' really do impact on the consciousness. My two-year-old grandson had a tantrum. After a very short time he stopped and said, "Well done, Finn, for stopping crying so quickly." Perhaps a unicorn nudged him.

We are all incredibly privileged to be incarnated on Earth at this time of opportunity for spiritual growth. There has never before been a period when so much assistance has been available from the spiritual realms and I offer you this little book on behalf of the unicorn kingdom with love.

The unicorns' message is:

When you focus on a vision beyond yourself we will assist you until your very essence blazes with light.

THE WAVE OF UNICORNS

S ince the first time a unicorn visited me there have been enormous changes on the planet. They are coming to Earth in a great wave to help us prepare for the new Golden Age.

In 2015, the extraordinary Archangel Christiel, who is in charge of the Unicorn Kingdom, was able to access this planet because our frequency had risen sufficiently by then. He sends fingers of light through the stargate of Lyra through the moon to Earth to allow unicorns to flood into Earth.

At the same time, since 2015 supermoons have bathed us powerfully in divine feminine energy and allowed even more unicorns to access our planet. These wondrous beings are literally pouring in during these full special times.

Many more of us have opened our twelve fifth-dimensional chakras and the unicorns are actively assisting us with this. As this has happened we have activated our causal chakra above our head. This is the spiritual centre through which we can connect with the angelic realms. And it is through this chakra that more unicorns can access Earth.

You can massively help the planetary ascension by working with your causal chakra! I discuss how the unicorns can enable you to do this and the new ninth- and tenth-dimensional frequency unicorns in my next book on unicorns. These illumined beings carry the Christ light and can take you to certain high-frequency places to bathe in pools of this pure love energy.

Preparing for the New Golden Age

The new Golden Age will start energetically in 2032. By that time the planet itself will be fully fifth-dimensional and so will most people and animals. Unicorns are helping us to reach that frequency in time. The process started at the cosmic moment in 2012. Many people had unrealistic expectations about what would happen then and thought everything would change in the twinkling of an eye—that, however, was never the intention. At 11.11 am on 21st December 2012, the cosmic clock struck. At that moment, the great pyramids in Mesopotamia, Greece, Tibet, Peru, South America and Egypt that are cosmic computers switched on. This was pre-programmed. They are to release information slowly over the following twenty years.

At the same moment, many portals and cosmic portals that were programmed to activate in 2012 started to wake up as well. This was the instant when the cosmic alarm roused them from a deep sleep. It will take most of them until 2032 to wake up fully.

It will be the same in 2032. The unicorns are encouraging and assisting as many people as possible to open and fully activate their twelve chakras by that time. When they are ready, only then can we bring Source light right down through our chakras into the Earth Star chakra below our feet. Then this light from Source is drawn by the archangels into the ley lines before it is directed to the pyramids. Even though most of these great structures have been physically destroyed, they are still working in the etheric.

By 2032, this higher light flowing through fifth-dimensional humans will energize the six cosmic pyramids. They will send the keys and codes out into the Universe to bring Earth into the correct alignment with the stars, so that our planet will fully ascend into the upper levels of the fifth dimension. We will take our rightful place in the Universe again.

As they did in the golden era of Atlantis, the unicorns will accompany those who are ready to visit other star systems in their physical bodies to bring back wisdom and advanced technology.

I have learnt much about these wondrous beings in the last few years. They are so much more than I understood when they first connected with me. Clearly I was like a kindergarten child and only given what I could comprehend at that time. As I have moved into more advanced classes, the unicorns have given me much more information which I will share in the sequel to this book.

Unicorns can transform your life on a personal level. They can also work with you to transform the world. I do hope you enjoy connecting with the unicorns and sending them to help others and the world.

I asked for a final message for this work and immediately felt pure white unicorn energy gathering behind me, which was a surprise. I usually see or feel one arriving in front of me. At last the message formed in my mind:

*Sense or picture our unicorn energy
surrounding you in white light.
Then you become like a pearl full of wisdom.
Our light enables you to release your wisdom
and be all you can be.
For this, stop doing and take time to be.
Remember that you are a cosmic being
and that we are all One.*

The Unicorns

ABOUT THE AUTHOR

Photo by Toby Phillips

Diana Cooper's spiritual journey started many years ago in the middle of a personal crisis, at the age of 42. She called out to the Universe for help and a golden angel appeared and took her on a journey to see her future.

Ten years later the angels reappeared and asked her to tell people about the angelic realms. When she finally agreed, they gave her information for her first angel book. After that they were with her all the time.

Diana has written more than 30 books and 11 card sets translated into 28 languages. She has travelled worldwide sharing information given to her by the angels, unicorns, dragons, and Illumined Ones.

She currently teaches a variety of online courses. Diana also founded the Diana Cooper School of White Light, a not-for-profit organization that offers certified spiritual teaching courses throughout the world.

For more information visit: **https://dianacooper.com**

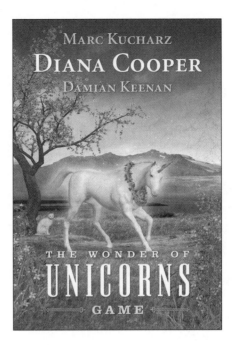

The Wonder of Unicorns Game
by Marc Kucharz, Diana Cooper, Damian Keenan

THE PURPOSE OF *The Wonder of Unicorns Game* is to enable players to be guided and feel supported to reach a specific goal by connecting to divine energy via the unicorns. Players need to be willing and ready to heal physical hurts, emotional traumas and spiritual wounds through the intercession of not only the unicorns' wisdom but also that of the other individual players.

Game elements include: 44 unicorn cards; a game rule booklet; a pad to take notes; 4 playing mats (game can be played with 1 to 4 players).

978-1-84409-676-3

FINDHORN PRESS

Life-Changing Books

Learn more about us and our books at
www.findhornpress.com

For information on the Findhorn Foundation:
www.findhorn.org